CRITICAL ACCLAIM
FOR GUTSY WOMEN

"Brimming with useful advice." —*San Francisco Examiner*

"Bond covers important subjects…with a lot of comforting information." —*Chicago Tribune*

"An invaluable pocket-sized guide for women who travel, whether you're headed for the wilderness or 5-star hotels." —*The Reader's Edge*

"The perfect bon voyage gift for your favorite woman traveler." —*Living Fit Magazine*

"A nuts-and-bolts approach to women's travel…seasoned advice geared both to novices and veterans." —*USA Today*

"A must-have for novice and experienced travelers alike. Packed with funny, instructive, and inspiring travel vignettes and tips for women on the road." —*Palo Alto Daily News*

"Packed with instructive and inspiring travel vignettes and tips…it is not just for adventure seekers or solo travelers." —*Boston Globe*

"How do you cope with an impulse to take wing? How do you handle desires to find adventures in exotic cultures…? If you're Marybeth Bond, you promptly leap aboard such urges, ride them where they happen to take you, then seek to lead others by word and example." —*San Francisco Chronicle*

"If you've got the bug to get out but are leery of the less-beaten path, check out *Gutsy Women*. Bond has packed this paperback with handy advice." —*Women's Sports & Fitness*

GUTSY WOMEN

more travel tips and wisdom for the road

GUTSY WOMEN

more travel tips and wisdom for the road

Second Edition

MARYBETH BOND

Travelers' Tales
San Francisco

Travelers' Tales and *Travelers' Tales Guides* are trademarks of Travelers' Tales, Inc., 330 Townsend Street, Suite 208, San Francisco, California 94107.
www.travelerstales.com

Cover design: Michele Wetherbee
Cover illustration: Melissa Sweet
Interior design: Susan Bailey
Research editors: Lisa Bach and Natanya Pearlman
Page layout: Cynthia Lamb using the fonts Berkeley Book, Wade Sans Light, and Gill Sans.

Distributed by Publishers Group West, 1700 Fourth Street, Berkeley, California 94710.

Library of Congress Cataloging-in-Publication Data

Bond, Marybeth.
    Gutsy women: more travel tips and wisdom for the road / by Marybeth Bond.
    —2nd ed.
      p. cm.
    ISBN 1-885211-61-9 (alk. paper)
    1. Travel. 2. Women travelers. I. Title.

  G151 .B66 2001
  910'.2'02—dc21   00-053681

Second Edition
Printed in the United States
10 9 8 7 6 5 4 3

For my parents, Ruth and Bill Bond;
my husband, Gary; and
my children, Julieclaire and Annalyse,
for encouraging me to fulfill my passion to travel—with and
without them.

TABLE OF CONTENTS

———

PREFACE TO THE SECOND EDITION

You gain strength, courage, and confidence by every experience in which you really stop to look fear in the face. You must do the thing which you think you cannot do.

—*Eleanor Roosevelt*

———

YOU ARE A GUTSY WOMAN. Just the fact that you bought a copy of *Gutsy Women* or someone thought you'd appreciate it as a gift means you have the characteristics of a Gutsy Woman. And what is a Gutsy Woman? She is open to adventure; seeks connections with people in other cultures; faces her fears; puts herself out there in the world; is transformed by travel. The tips and wisdom that fill the pages of this edition of *Gutsy Women* will inspire and energize, illuminate and empower. Even if you never knew you were a Gutsy Woman, this book will allow you to discover her within yourself.

Years ago women traveled very differently than they do today. Women used to travel, primarily with their families or their husbands, to limited destinations on orchestrated tours on land or on cruise ships. But now more and more women are getting off the beaten track and wandering the globe, either on their own or with other women. If your husband or partner isn't interested in traveling, then I encourage you to find friends who are. If friends are too busy and you feel compelled to travel, then simply plan a journey of your own. You may be frightened by this idea, but if you read *Gutsy Women* and arm yourself with its wisdom, you will be more prepared for your transformative journey. Your first trip as a Gutsy Woman doesn't have to be to the other side of the world. It can be a journey close to home—just so you can get your travel feet wet. Even if you are already a seasoned traveler, I'm sure you will learn something new and useful in this revised and expanded edition of *Gutsy Women*.

Over the past two decades I have hiked, cycled, climbed, dived, and kayaked my way through more than seventy countries, from the depths of the Flores Sea to the summit of Mount Kilimanjaro. I traveled alone around the world for two years at the age of twenty-nine; in recent years I have traveled with my husband and two children, and I continue to travel with women's groups, girlfriends, my mother, and alone. I travel all over the world speaking to women about their experiences on the road. I've shared a lot of useful information and have met many incredible women who share their lives, travels, and tips with me. It is my hope that reading *Gutsy Women* will encourage you in your travels. The information you will find within this new edition speaks to a much broader experience of women travelers. I've updated the tips and added many more—making sure to include the most useful information to help you prepare for your trip and ensure you have a safe and adventurous journey.

The wisdom in this book is for women of all ages. Whether you are a maiden voyager at age eighteen or eighty or a seasoned world traveler, you will discover that women help and inspire each other while on the road. Seek out the community of women—a worldwide network exists—and know that these new connections will enhance your travels. I hope that my extensive travel experience guides and motivates you in your journeys.

Gutsy Women—go forth and change yourselves and the world.

INTRODUCTION
WHAT IS A GUTSY WOMAN?

Travel not only stirs the blood...it also gives birth to the spirit.
—*Alexandra David-Neel, French explorer, writer (1868–1969)*

———

SOMEONE ONCE TOLD ME we live our lives one of three ways: treadmill, saga, or pilgrimage. Take your pick, she said, for it is a choice you must make every day.

To avoid a saga in my own life and to get off the treadmill, I often feel the need to hit the road. I create pilgrimages for myself, from an afternoon hike or an overnight trip to an extended journey anywhere outside my zip code.

Am I frightened to travel? It depends. When I go on an organized tour—never. When I am freewheeling with my husband—rarely. When I travel alone with my children—sometimes. And when I go solo—always! So why do I put myself through this?

Fear and discomfort about traveling diminishes with time and experience. Taking one small risk leads to taking larger risks until you realize you have made leaps of confidence and you are a competent traveler. More women are taking that first step every day.

In the next few years, women will comprise more than half of all business travelers, compared with only 1 percent in 1970. Over 70 percent of organized adventure travel clients are women. Women also account for $55 billion in retail sales of travel equipment. Women are responsible for making more than 70 percent of the decisions for all types of travel, and they are spending more discretionary income on travel. Everyone is waking up to women's buying power as more women of all ages take to the road.

After the publication of my first book *A Woman's World*, a collection of women's travel writing, I traveled nationwide on a book tour. From college students hitting the road for the first time to mature widows just beginning to spread their wings, women of all ages and levels of experience asked me for advice. Seasoned travelers in the audience shared their tried-and-true tips, too.

Men, especially talk-show hosts, focused on the safety issue: "Weren't you concerned for your safety? Isn't travel risky? What about rape? What was your worst experience?"

Women more often asked: "How do you carry your money? How do you pack lightly? What's it like eating alone in a restaurant? Are there countries women traveling alone should avoid? What are your tips for meeting people? How do you arrange visits in local homes and schools? What do you do on bad hair days, when you've been in remote areas and were unable to bathe? Did you get sick? What's the best preventive medicine? Is there anywhere you can't buy tampons? What about condoms?"

Gutsy Women is an attempt to answer these questions, open doors for the novice, and share advice across generations, among peers. This is a book of travel tips and wisdom, but, like my other books, *A Woman's World, A Mother's World,* and *A Woman's Passion for Travel,* it is about more than just travel. It is about the rewards of risk-taking, living, feeling, learning, and loving; it is about having the strength to be ourselves and taking steps toward making our dreams real.

Women are unique in many ways—our views of the world, our approaches to life, our expressions of freedom. Relationships are important to us and we make connections quickly and easily. We also have unique concerns and issues. Safety and security are at the top of the list, and we are arming ourselves with the knowledge and skills to avoid and survive dangerous situations. Is travel a risky business? Yes, but all of life is risky. We live in an unsafe country. And yet we have learned to cope and take care of ourselves in this environment. Following these same instincts in foreign countries will protect us.

By age twenty-nine I had already lived and traveled overseas for six years. But my appetite for travel was not satisfied, so I made preparations to take off and travel alone around the world. "You have good sense, Marybeth, please use it," my mother urged me. She also asked that I promise not to take any drugs that would cloud my ability to make wise decisions. My father asked me to promise that I would carry enough money on me at all times to take a taxi, even a few blocks, to avoid dangerous situations after dark. I followed their advice.

Considering how much I have traveled over the past three decades—from Kathmandu to Killarney, from Ecuador to Tanzania—and considering how often I have traveled alone and stayed in very modest accommodations, I have had very few threatening experiences. I have asked for help when I needed it; I've followed my instincts and the advice of seasoned travelers. I've had remarkable adventures.

In the pages that follow you'll encounter words of wisdom from a multitude of experienced women travelers that will help you on your way, confirm your own instincts, or inspire new ideas about traveling in our world. At the back of the book are resources that will help answer your more specific questions, as well as a reading list to enhance your preparation.

Many Gutsy Women are already traveling, are on the road as you read this. And many more need only a word or two of encouragement to step out the door. Remember, you only need three things to have a great trip: your passport, your money, and, above all, your sense of humor. Bon voyage.

1
THE FIRST STEP

The impulse to travel is one of the hopeful symptoms of life.
—*Agnes Repplier*

———

BEFORE WE DO ANYTHING IN LIFE, even the most impulsive of us do some preparation. We educate ourselves to prepare for careers, plan strategies for important meetings, make menus for simple or extravagant meals. Preparation helps us reduce fears by giving us knowledge and builds confidence by increasing our comfort with the unknown.

Preparing yourself mentally and emotionally for traveling overseas is just as important as getting your visas and shots. Give yourself time to work through fears you may have about safety, traveling alone or in a group of unknown companions, or fitting into a different culture. To convert your apprehension into excitement, begin your mental preparation weeks or even months prior to departure. Get in touch with women who have gone before you. They will be your role models. Connect with them by phone, e-mail, or by reading their stories in travel books.

It is reassuring before you take your trip to have a complete itinerary, guidebooks, research from the Internet, and detailed notes from friends who have been there before. I've found that the most valuable sources of up-to-date information are other travelers you'll meet along the way, locals you will encounter on trains or at bus stops, or the staff

> Travel invigorates the mind like physical exercise invigorates the body. It keeps our senses alert and allows instinct to flower, which is our greatest guide.
>
> ◆
>
> *Arlene Chester Burns, 36, reporter for ESPN*

at tourist offices, hotels, and bed-and-breakfasts. Fight the urge to organize everything before you go. Spontaneity and flexibility are the creative forces behind meaningful journeys. Try to avoid overscheduling and overplanning.

When I left on my around-the-world journey, I had a detailed itinerary. I abandoned it on day three in Bangkok. If I had followed my original plans, I never would have met Danielle, a Swiss nurse with whom I traveled for a month, stayed with a Muslim family on a houseboat in Kashmir, or hiked for a week with another new travel friend among the ethnic tribes of northern Thailand. It is tempting to follow a structured itinerary on long or short trips. Recently, on a weeklong trip to Paris, I lost all the notes a friend gave me with restaurant and shopping recommendations. Instead of reliving her trip, I discovered my own, more relaxed version of the City of Lights. I dined *en plein air* at a sidewalk restaurant on the seventeenth-century Place des Vosges and visited three museums in one day, instead of searching for my friend's favorite shops.

We discover the world as we physically move around the planet; we discover ourselves on the inner journey that accompanies our travels. The rewards are many: We try on new identities as more independent, self-sufficient women; we explore new behaviors; and we develop a greater awareness of our potential.

> The trick is not to rid your stomach of butterflies, but to make them fly in formation.
>
> ◆
>
> *Pacific Crest Outward Bound School*, Book of Readings

Remind yourself that the minimal risk of traveling is far outweighed by the rewards.

TIPS

➤ Buy your airline tickets on a Wednesday. Although it is not always the case, here's the typical scenario: An airline announces a fare sale on Monday, and on Tuesday other airlines match the price or undercut it. On Wednesday, the fare war is in high gear. By Thursday most of the cheap fares are gone. Saturday is the worst day to buy a ticket. Airlines usually raise their prices late on Friday night to see if other airlines will, too. If no one follows suit, then fares may go back down by Monday.

➢ Do your research. Begin at your public library or on-line. Search by subject matter or country name for a listing of all magazine and newspaper articles, historical and political studies, novels, documentaries, and movies about the destination you are visiting. Check out books or videos well in advance of your journey.

> ____ ⋰⋰ ____
>
> As a woman, my fear of being cooped up in my home without new challenges, new conversations, new vistas, far outweighs any fears I might have of traveling solo in a strange land.
>
> ◆
>
> *Evelyn Hannon, 56,*
> *editor,* Journeywoman,
> *Toronto, Canada*

➢ Put travel anthologies on your reading list, including books by and about women and collections that focus on the countries you want to visit. The Travelers' Tales series is a superb place to start.

➢ Spend time in a specialized travel bookstore in your hometown or make an effort to visit one online. Try Book Passage (www.bookpassage.com), located near San Francisco, or the Savvy Traveler (www.thesavvytraveller.com) in Chicago. You'll be carried away by the depth of available travel titles. You can also find extensive travel collections at the Tattered Cover (www.tatteredcover.com) in Denver or Powell's (www.powells.com) in Portland.

➢ Seek out people who have traveled or lived in the country you'll be visiting and ask them lots of questions, especially about good reading material and whether they know citizens from there now living in the U.S.

➢ Get on the Internet and browse through the travel chat rooms and especially the news groups. You may make contact with interesting people from the country where you plan to travel. Often when you arrive you'll have a name and phone number of someone to look up.

➤ The local embassy or consulate can provide answers to general questions and will provide reading material upon request.

➤ Learn a few words in the local language—hello, good-bye, please, thank you, beautiful. If you have the time, take a language course.

➤ Get to know a good travel agent. You will never regret it, no matter how adept you become at your own trip planning and online ticket purchasing.

> _——— ⋅⋅⋅ぃ⋅⋅ ———_
>
> When I travel I take two journeys—the outward and the inward journey. When I push myself I expand my borders and possibilities. I reach beyond my limits.
>
> ◆
>
> *Lynne Cox, 39, first person to swim across the Bering Strait, Los Alamitos, California*

➤ It's easy to book a package deal—including airfare, hotel, and car rental—and there are good reasons to do so. You know you'll have no big surprises and peace of mind.

➤ Stay at a family-run guesthouse or bed-and-breakfast. Local families in many countries treat their guests like long-lost relatives. They'll cook local specialties for you, play their music, and share their evenings with you. If you join Servas you'll stay in private homes with locals who want to host you. See the Resources section for more details.

➤ Eat out at a local restaurant that serves authentic food from the country you plan to visit. Chances are that the owners or staff are expatriates and can provide valuable information.

➤ Fuel your passion by planning your trip around a special interest such as art, cooking, biking, gardening, etc. If you love gardening, do targeted online research to find famous gardens you can visit at your destination, whether it is in England, India, or Japan. Contact the local tourist bureau and ask if there are historic house tours, kitchen tours, or garden tours you can take. Consider taking a cooking class in Italy, France, or Thailand. Local organizations may be able to provide helpful information about these activities at your destination. You will meet other like-minded individuals if you pursue your interests while traveling.

I never regretted any trip I took, no matter how inconvenient, expensive, or unnecessary it seemed at the planning stage. I only regretted the trips I didn't take.

♦

Carol Benet, Ph.D. 57, art critic, teacher, and counselor, U.C. Berkeley, Belvedere, California

➤ Consider doing some volunteer work as part of your travels. Getting involved in volunteer organizations offers a great opportunity to deepen your experience and helps you get beneath the surface of a culture. See Chapter XVIII for more information.

I like the feeling when I'm traveling that I am responsible only for myself and my few possessions. In some ways I am in complete control of everything I do. In other ways, I have no choice but to surrender myself to the hands of the fates. The blending of these two states is romantic, enchanting, intoxicating.

♦

Laurie Armstrong, 37, vice president, San Francisco Convention and Visitors Bureau

II
PREPARATION FOR DEPARTURE AND ARRIVAL

Is there anything as horrible as starting on a trip? Once you're off, that's all right, but the last moments are earthquake and convulsion, and the feeling that you are a snail being pulled off your rock.

—*Anne Morrow Lindbergh,* Gift from the Sea

EVEN THOUGH YOU MAY BE very nervous about traveling, if it doesn't turn out to be what you expected, you can always go home. You always have this safety net. And if you feel like there is a lot of pressure to continue, you can simply change your plans en route. You may decide, for example, to skip India and head straight for Thailand. It is your trip and you make the decisions.

I give myself a pep talk: *Get ready, things will be different where you are traveling. Don't expect to have as much control as you have at home. You can expect to be uncomfortable at times, delayed often, bored occasionally, and most certainly frustrated.* Departure is as easy as stepping off a curb—if you know it is there and prepare.

To prepare myself for an upcoming trip, especially if it's to the developing world, I make a personal (and private) ritual to say good-bye to my favorite comforts and foods at home—like my soft pillow, fresh salads, and clean running water. I remind myself that these luxuries await me upon my return and that I must try to

> There is one priceless thing that I brought back from my trip around the world, one that cost no money and on which I paid no customs duty: humility, a humility born from watching other peoples, other races, struggling bravely and hoping humbly for the simplest things in life.
>
> ◆
>
> *Felix Marti-Ibanez,*
> Journey around Myself

be tolerant of discomfort, unfamiliar food, and different concepts of time and personal space.

Even experienced travelers often forget that culture shock can be most intense when you return home. You may be astonished at what you see during your travels, but it is often not until your return home that shock settles in or has the room to make itself known to you. Take baths and walks, indulge yourself with the gift of time if you can. Let your digestive system readjust to what was once familiar food. Let your system integrate the experiences you've had.

When I returned from two years of travel, mostly in developing countries, my first trip to the supermarket was overwhelming. I just walked up and down the aisles, amazed at the choices. Immobilized by the bounty, unable to make any decisions, I left the store empty-handed. Common activities like driving a car or listening to my friends complain about their lives were difficult to handle. It is important to come home with an open mind to the life you left behind, because inevitably you return with a different perspective. Ease your way back into home life.

TIPS

➤ To avoid feeling overwhelmed by your impending departure, allow enough time to prepare, logistically and mentally.

➤ You will greatly reduce the stress associated with your departure if you begin packing several days in advance. You will then have time to mend favorite clothes or wash dirty ones before taking off.

> Why am I doing this? I came to realize that there were many reasons.... I believe that life is to be lived fully. When an opportunity arises…go for it.
>
> ♦
>
> *Anne Dal Vera, 42,*
> *explorer, Frisco, Colorado*

➤ Checklists can be handy for keeping track of packing, good-byes to friends, closing up the house, canceling the newspaper, and other necessary tasks.

➤ Take along personal photos of your friends, family, and pets. This will be a wonderful reminder of those you love.

➤ Prebook your first night's accommodation. Chances are you'll feel more comfortable in a new environment if you have a plan— where you're going (hotel, guest house, youth hostel) and how you'll get there (taxi, public transportation, rental car).

➤ When you phone or fax the establishment of your first night's stay, ask if they offer a shuttle from the airport. If not, what should a taxi cost? Is there a convenient, safe local bus or sub-way? Can they recommend a local car rental agency? (They are often less expensive than national chains.) Find answers to these questions and you'll arrive more confident and know how to proceed.

➤ Pack lightly. If you cannot carry your bag from your bedroom to the car when you are leaving, you know you will have trouble carrying it from the taxi to the lobby of your hotel or from the train platform to your train compartment. Most travelers worry about handling their luggage, so rethink what you've packed and lighten up!

➤ Depending on your personality, you may want to take it easy the day you arrive. Allow free time for a bath, nap, or unstruc-tured exploration.

➤ Soon after your arrival, find a café or restaurant for what I call my "observation ritual." Sit and watch. Take specific note of the dress and behavior of women. If women don't expose their legs or arms or head, you should quickly follow suit and cover up. If they avoid eye contact, smiling, or conversations with men, be forewarned of how Western behavior may be interpreted.

➤ If you are traveling alone or are the least bit anxious about travel in the country of your choice, consider finding, upon arrival, a woman at the airport who is leaving the country. Ask her specific questions, such as: Is there any place that is not safe? Is there a place where Western travelers hang out and exchange information? Are there any sights, markets, or restaurants she'd highly recommend?

➢ To stay calm on the day of your departure, give yourself plenty of time to get to the airport, train, or bus station. Be packed and ready to go the night before.

➢ Be easy on yourself when you get back from a trip.

➢ Give yourself time to reacclimatize to your old world and make it your own again.

_____ ⁄⁄⁄ _____

We generate fears while we sit; we overcome them by action. Fear is nature's warning signal to get busy.

◆

Pacific Crest Outward Bound School, Book of Readings

III
SAFETY AND SECURITY

Intuition and instinct are the best protectors for a woman.
—*Sheila Swan,* Safety & Security for Women Who Travel

THE MOMENT WE STEP OUT the door, we are aware of the footsteps behind us. We are concerned for our personal safety and with good reason. Safety and security are primary concerns for women, especially those traveling to unfamiliar places. To travel without fear, we need to arm ourselves with knowledge, preparedness, awareness, and a flexible attitude.

We can avoid questionable neighborhoods. We can communicate that we are self-assured by walking confidently with our heads up, aware of our surroundings. When traveling alone we can avoid countries where the men are known for hassling women, such as certain Islamic countries and areas of southern Europe. If we apply the common sense we use at home, we can feel safe virtually anywhere.

> Courage is not freedom from fear; it is being afraid and going on. Once you have looked fear in the face and have overcome it, you can do it again and again and again.
>
> ◆
>
> *Pacific Crest Outward Bound School,* Book of Readings

The following tips are intended to increase your awareness, comfort level, and power to travel safely. One thing is certain: The more you travel the less fear you will experience. When in doubt, ask a lot of questions or ask for help.

If you are still concerned, tell yourself that you are a Gutsy Woman and that is, in fact, what you will become.

GENERAL SAFETY TIPS

➢ Use the common sense you've honed over the years. If you

wouldn't walk in an unknown neighborhood after dark at home, do not do it overseas.

➤ Trust your instincts. Let me repeat that: Trust your instincts. Instincts are not a matter of consensus. If you feel something is off, wrong, strange—get out, move on, flee, whatever is appropriate. Do it quickly.

➤ It is common for a would-be thief to use razor blades to cut purse straps, take the purse, and then get away in a thick sea of bodies. Wear a money belt to prevent this from happening.

➤ Carry all valuables, including airline or train tickets, money, passports, etc., in a money belt under your clothes. Keep only what you need for the day in your pocket or daypack.

> ———— ⚜ ————
>
> Use your city smarts. Try to avoid potentially dicey places like a deserted street in a big city. If you are alone, don't walk down it. Having other people around is your best safety insurance.
>
> ◆
>
> *Susan Spano, 46,*
> Los Angeles Times *staff writer,*
> *Los Angeles, California*

➤ If you plan on staying in hostels, carry a combination lock with you to secure your backpack to your bed or in a locker if you are leaving your room. It is also useful to attach your backpack to the luggage rack in a train compartment.

➤ Let your family, friends, or embassy know your trip itinerary if you are going somewhere unusual or potentially dangerous.

➤ It can be very difficult to know what is considered offensive or suggestive in segregated societies, such as orthodox Muslim areas. At times you may feel uncomfortable or vulnerable. You may not know if the local men view you as a sex symbol or immoral. So take your cues from the local women. Blend in. Dress appropriately. Ask other Western women who have experience in this culture for their advice.

➤ Use your judgment at public demonstrations or political rallies with massive crowds. Sometimes they can become violent and should be avoided, while other times attending such gatherings can be enlightening. If you have doubts, stay near the edge of the crowd.

➤ If you have to wait somewhere, look for other women or families to sit with. If you are seated with someone, it is unlikely that you will be approached or harassed. Ask for help or company if you feel uncomfortable.

> ———— \\\\// ————
>
> Definitely take a self-defense course and never let your guard down. Then you'll feel like you can enjoy the trip.
>
> ◆
>
> *Elizabeth Harryman, 40,*
> *radio broadcaster,*
> *Los Angeles, California*

➤ If a group of men or young boys approaches you on the sidewalk, cross to the other side of the street to give them space and you peace of mind.

➤ If you are being followed on the street and you feel threatened, duck into a shop and firmly tell the clerk: "I am a foreigner and someone is following me. I am frightened and need help." If need be, have the clerk call a taxi or the police for you.

➤ Always carry enough money in your shoe to get you out of a tight spot. Be willing to spend this money on a cab in order to get you to a safe place or back to your lodging. Do not take unnecessary risks.

➤ Scam artists such as thieves and pickpockets create distractions as a cover-up. Beware of people who accidentally spill something on your clothing, bump into you, or drop a piece of luggage in front of you. This is the time to watch your luggage and keep a hand on your valuables. Don't underestimate the skill of rip-off artists—they can misdirect your attention no matter how watchful you are.

- ➤ Study a map before you leave your lodging or car so that once on the street you know where you are headed. Try to avoid struggling with a map or looking like a tourist.

- ➤ Dress down when you travel. Avoid wearing jewelry—even jewelry that is cheap but looks expensive.

- ➤ Stay alert when getting off a bus or train or riding an escalator, as this is when pickpockets tend to strike.

- ➤ If you must ask for directions, approach women with children or families.

- ➤ Serendipity is at the heart of all travel. Once you are on the road, if you take small risks such as talking to a local person or accepting an invitation to someone's home, often your reward will be experiences you will long remember.

- ➤ Avoid having your luggage accidentally taken by identifying it with a personal touch—a colorful luggage tag, a unique ribbon around the handle, or a guitar strap or specially made luggage band.

_____ ⎠⎠⎠ _____

Clothing that is fashionable and appropriate at home may project a provocative image in another culture. Leave the revealing clothing behind.

◆

MBB

_____ ⎠⎠⎠ _____

Once in Old Delhi, my girlfriend and I lost our guide and thus our ride. We realized we also had no cash. What were we going to do, cry? No. We sat down and laughed. We wandered through dark back alleys, past men pissing in corners, until we found a fancy English bank, but they couldn't give us cash from our credit cards or travelers checks. An Indian executive of the bank insisted he give us enough rupees to get us to the money exchange office. The moral of the story? Don't be shy. Trust people. Ask people. Get up and go.

◆

Lenore Thornton, 51,
investment advisor,
New York City

➤ Be sure to know when the sun sets. A bustling market can quickly empty out and be transformed into dark, deserted streets. Plan to be back to your lodging or in a safe, busy neighborhood by dark.

➤ Traveling internationally, learn how to dial for police, fire, abulance—and your nation's consulate or embassy. Put the latter in your passport on a piece of paper with instructions in the local language explaining who to call, your blood type, any serious allergies to medicines.

ROAD TRIP SAFETY TIPS

➤ Plan your driving time during daylight hours and lock your doors when you get into your vehicle.

➤ When entering your car, be aware, look around you, and look into your car. Before you get into your vehicle, make sure no one is hiding inside.

➤ If you are parked next to a van, enter your car from the door opposite where the van is parked. Many serial killers attack their victims by pulling them into their vans.

➤ Do not enter your car if a car is parked next to it with someone sitting inside. It's always better to be safe than sorry. Do not hesitate to ask a guard or policeman to escort you to your car.

➤ As soon as you enter your automobile, lock the doors. Do not sit in a parking lot and eat, work, or sleep. This makes you a target.

➤ Restrooms at truck stops, gas stations, and public rest stops can be unsafe. Stop at moderate hotels that are likely to have a lobby, as they will usually have a clean and safe public restroom and other amenities like phones, soft drink machines, newspaper dispensers.

➤ Crime in airport parking lots is increasing. Pay attention to where you park—look for parking spaces under lights, close to the terminal. Often the "off-airport" lots are safer. The shuttle bus picks you up at your car, takes you to the terminal, and drops you off at your car again. If it is dark and you feel uncomfortable, ask the driver to wait until you are safely inside your car.

➤ When you rent a car, ask for an up-to-date map and directions to your first meeting or hotel. Be sure to ask which neighborhoods can be dangerous and should be avoided. With the help of the rental car representative, cross off the dangerous areas on your map, so you don't accidentally drive through or stop in an unsafe area.

➤ If someone yells or honks at you, indicates that there is something wrong, or bumps your car while you are driving, do not stop. Drive to a well-lit, busy place and then check it out.

➤ If you are not already a member of the American Automobile Association (AAA), join before you take a long road trip. Their roadside assistance is invaluable.

➤ Be sure your spare tire is inflated and that you know how to change it. For added security, always carry a can of "Fix a Flat" spray in the trunk.

➤ If you don't own a cell phone, consider borrowing or buying one for your trip. Program 911 into the automatic dial feature.

LODGING TIPS

➤ When you check in, register using your last name and your first initial only. Also ask that your room number not be announced. If they say your room number aloud, ask to be put in another room.

➤ At check-in, request a room on the second to the sixth floors. Thieves target rooms on the ground level with easy escape access, and some fire hoses cannot reach above the sixth floor.

➢ Hang out the "Do Not Disturb" sign and leave the TV on when you leave your room. This will discourage anyone from entering your room while you are away.

➢ Always remember to carry your key with you at all times. Be careful not to leave a spare key in your room, even if it doesn't have your room number on it. If it is stolen from your room, the thief knows where to return.

➢ Always place your room key in the same location. In the event of an emergency, you will want to have time to take the key with you, allowing for your quick return if it was only a fire drill. You don't want to be caught in the hallway in a skimpy nightgown and then have to wait at the front desk for another key to be issued. Leave it on the television or on the bedside table.

➢ Carry a rubber doorstop in your luggage. This provides added security in your hotel room. Use it either on the main door or an adjoining room door that may not have double locks. Keep it in your suitcase and don't unpack it between trips.

➢ Always secure all of the locks on hotel room doors whenever you are in the room. It is essential for your protection. You could be in the bathroom and not hear someone knock. You don't want anyone to enter the room while you are inside, even to check the mini-bar or turn down your sheets.

➢ Play it safe and avoid displaying your hotel room key in public. Don't leave it on your restaurant table or on the chair by the swimming pool—it could be stolen or someone could read the name of your hotel and your room number.

➢ If someone knocks on your hotel room door, verify who it is. If there is a peephole, use it. If the person identifies him- or herself as a hotel employee, request that they come back later, when you've left the room. If they insist on entering, call the front desk and confirm that someone from the staff needs to enter your room and for what purpose before letting anyone in.

➤ If you fill out the room service breakfast order form that you hang on your door after hours, do not divulge your first name (which indicates you are female) or the number of people eating. This advertises that you are a woman and alone for the night.

➤ Request a room near the elevators and away from any renovation work. Have your key out when you leave the elevator.

➤ Lock valuables in a safe at the front desk or in your room—even while you are in the shower.

➤ If your bag is stolen from the hotel, recruit management to search for it. Most hotel robberies are committed by staff members. Many hotels do not let their staff leave with packages, so the thieves often take the money and dump the rest on the premises.

➤ When choosing a hotel, smaller is sometimes smarter: You want the staff to recognize guests and be more familiar with you. The smaller the lobby, the more noticeable loiterers become.

➤ Inquire when you book if there is sufficient staff to walk you to your room late at night. This will give you an idea of how woman-friendly the hotel is.

During one recent hotel stay, I checked into a sixth-floor room that had curtains fluttering at two open windows. I didn't think anything of it—until I woke up in the morning to see the silhouette of a man standing right behind one of them! I screamed, ran to the bathroom, and locked myself in. When I peeked out, the man was gone. I walked over to the window, looked out and realized that a fire escape was right outside. Now I always check for fire escapes when I check into a room.

◆

Janet Fullwood, 47, travel editor, Sacramento Bee, *Sacramento, California*

IV
KEEPING IN TOUCH

I send my words into the world and wait
for whatever new words will come.
—*Georgia Heard,* Writing Toward Home

AFTER SAFETY, ACCORDING TO STUDIES AND POLLS conducted by hotel chains and travel publications, the second most important concern for women travelers is keeping in touch. I agree.

Depending upon where you are going and how long you are staying, keeping in touch with home may be as simple as making a phone call or sending an e-mail or fax. If you are planning a trip of a month or longer—especially in developing countries—you'll need to figure out how and if you can receive mail, and you'll need to alert your family and friends. You'll also need to prepare yourself to live comfortably without correspondence from home for periods of time.

If you travel to a technologically remote country, the best methods for communicating easily with home are faxes and telegrams. It's true, post offices in physically remote regions still send telegrams. When Western Union receives your message in the USA, they will call the recipient by phone and mail a copy of your message. From Morocco, Ireland, or Ecuador, I could easily send and receive a one-page fax every week. This is easy to do

Before I left home I asked my family to make me a tape of their favorite music. Each member contributed a piece to the tape. I have everything from Mozart to the Eagles to kids songs by Raffi. Whenever I was apprehensive, I could play the tape and feel grounded.

◆

*Rosemarie Enslin, 51, president,
Enslin Associates, Calgary,
Alberta, Canada*

from the hotel office in most cities. When my children send a fax to me, they draw pictures and tell me all the little details of their day-today lives. Why do I prefer fax communication to telephones? First, you don't have to deal with time differences. Second, it is much less expensive. Third, and most important, you do not take the chance of catching a loved one in a grumpy mood (or just tired) and thus finishing the phone conversation with a sense of disappointment or anxiety. An extra emotional benefit is keeping and rereading a fax sent from home.

Today, cybercafés are popping up all over the world, from ice cream shops in San Miguel, Mexico, to local bars in small French villages. Internet access is even available in some more remote locations like northern Thailand or on the island of Tonga. Getting online is becoming less expensive and more accessible worldwide. So do not hesitate to stay in touch with your loved ones by e-mail. It is also handy if you need to download maps or do more research on the town you are in.

TIPS

➢ Be sure to pack a copy of your address book. Do not take your original.

➢ Set up an e-mail account with Hotmail, AOL, or Yahoo! It will be easy for you to check your e-mail if you can access your account through a Web-based service provider.

➢ E-mail is an excellent way to stay in touch. Check with other travelers or the desk clerk at your lodging to find the closest cybercafé. If you want to locate Internet cafés before you leave, try www.netcafeguide.com for a database of locations.

I began a tradition on my first trip overseas that I still practice today, sixteen years later: keeping a journal. I write as though I am penning a letter to my mother, complete with all the silly details I know she loves (like what kinds of pastries I've devoured and about my room's mismatched wallpaper). Rereading my journals is like taking a trip back in time—one much more vivid than memory alone can inspire. And for a solo traveler, it gives you something to do while you're waiting for food in restaurants.

◆

Katy Koontz, 37, freelance travel writer, Knoxville, Tennessee

➤ Many people still prefer communicating home by telephone. There are so many telephone company and card options now that even a simple long-distance call can be complicated. Know how to use your phone card to make long-distance calls before you leave on a trip and keep the access number for your long distance carrier in an easy-to-locate place in your address book.

➤ Avoid being overcharged by using in-room hotel phones. There are companies that now offer a callback service. Once you are registered, you simply call and enter the hotel phone number where you will be staying. At your destination, when you want to make a call, dial a special number, let it ring once, and hang up. The service will automatically call you back at your hotel (a computer-ized voice will ask for you by name). Then, once you enter your special access code, you are free to start making your calls. For now, at least, hotels don't charge for incoming calls.

———— ⋇ ————

When I arrived at my hotel room in Marrakech I placed a framed picture of my daughters on the bedside table. When I returned from visiting the bustling medinas later in the day, I found fresh flowers arranged around the picture. This touching ritual continued mysteriously for two days before the maid caught me in the hall, followed me to my room, picked up my picture, kissed the photo of my girls, and through gestures told me about her own family.

◆

MBB

➤ Give a detailed itinerary to loved ones before you leave and include the fax numbers for your hotels or accommodations. Then ask your family or friends to fax you once or twice during your trip.

➤ If your journey is going to be unstructured and spontaneous, send postcards, e-mails, or faxes to keep people up to date as your plans develop, should there be an emergency at home.

➤ If you are going on an extended trip, find a good, organized, reliable friend to handle your correspondence. We have friends who are currently sailing around the world for several years. Although I have their rough itinerary, they have altered their plans numerous times and I can only guess how long it will take my letters to reach them. But I can easily send a letter, fax, or postcard to the person who is in charge of their affairs. She handles all of their mail, knows where they are, more or less, and forwards mail to them.

➤ When I was traveling in remote areas without telephone service, I sent telegrams home regularly. If you keep it short, they are not expensive.

➤ You can receive mail worldwide at poste restante, or general delivery, at the main post office in town. Most guidebooks can give you addresses. Your mail will be held for one month.

➤ You may prefer to have mail sent to the "Client Letter Service" at American Express offices in developing countries because they tend to be more reliable than post offices. Of course, you must have an American Express credit card or traveler's checks. American Express will provide you with a list of worldwide mailing addresses.

➤ Advise your friends and family to address your letters clearly, avoiding cursive writing. When you go to collect mail, check under both your first and last names.

➤ Send yourself or bring home the most beautiful postcards you find. I love to display them in my office as a fond reminder of the "other me."

➤ To stay in touch with yourself, keep a journal.

When I was traveling for two years, I took along a small tape recorder and empty cassettes. I taped letters to my parents as I traveled and sent them home every few weeks. They sent me long tapes, too. I particularly loved the tapes recorded at family reunions, complete with greetings from aunts, uncles, and little cousins.

◆

MBB

V

HEALTH AND HYGIENE
ON THE ROAD

Health is not a condition of matter, but of mind.
—*Mary Baker Eddy, founder, Christian Science Church*

WHEN I RETURN FROM AN EXOTIC PLACE, the first thing many people ask me is "Did you get sick?" They want to know, specifically, if I got traveler's diarrhea. Yes, that is my most common travel-related illness. To avoid it, be very careful about what you eat and drink. Eating dairy products is a hit-or-miss affair. You wouldn't want to pass up creamy pastries in Paris or gelato in Italy, but you will need to think twice before eating the same products in a developing country where refrigeration, sanitation, and pasteurization is spotty.

What about eating at food stalls? You have to take a few chances to have some wonderful culinary encounters and, yes, even risk getting sick. In Southeast Asia some of the best food available is found in the street stalls. You'll have to do some investigating, though. Ask other travelers and locals where it is safe to eat. Look for crowded places.

If you plan to travel to remote areas, take along an emergency medical kit that can be used by

---

\\\\//

I always pack a low-fat, high-energy snack, because I get off the plane and start running (or hiking) immediately. It includes low-fat crackers, dry soup mixes, low-fat hot chocolate, carrot and celery sticks, a green apple, and always, always, a container of Grey Poupon mustard. It is great on apples. I usually carry a loaf of French bread too. If you get in late and nothing is open, you're all set. Pack an immersion coil (you can buy one at a hardware store) so you can boil water.

♦

Carole Jacobs, 40+, travel editor, Shape *magazine, Woodland Hills, California*

health personnel. Include in it sterile syringes, needles, dressings, and gloves. I travel with my own individually wrapped sterile syringes. Once, after traveling for about nine months, I thought I might need another dose of gamma globulin. I was in Kathmandu at the time and although I went to a Red Cross facility, I was very pleased to hand the nurse my sterile syringe. Before my extended travels, I asked a nurse friend to prepare an official document, on her medical stationery, listing all the prescription drugs, medicines, and syringes that were in my medical kit. While I never needed this document, I was prepared for a thorough border search. Preparation and precaution will help you stay healthy.

TIPS

➢ Build up your immune system before you go by taking vitamins. You may be eating irregular meals and less nutritious food while on the road, so take along vitamins to supplement your diet.

➢ In countries with questionable sanitation, don't drink the water. Don't brush your teeth with tap water, rinse your mouth in the shower, or put ice cubes in your drinks. Drink only bottled or treated water. Don't accept bottled water unless you see it opened in your presence. Eat only salads and fruit that you have prepared and peeled yourself.

> On a monthlong trek in the Himalayas, the most appreciated gift I shared with fellow trekkers was the use of my sunscreen and Chapstick. My lips seem to dry out and crack from the moment I step on the plane.
>
> ◆
>
> *MBB*

➢ I swear by Pepto Bismol and Alka Seltzer tablets. I recommend you pack an ample supply.

➢ If you get diarrhea, consume fluids, eat bland, dry foods, and rest. Consider short-term use of Imodium or Ciprofloxacin. I always travel with Ciprofloxacin, which is a fabulous all-purpose antibiotic that can be used for upper respiratory problems or serious traveler's diarrhea. You'll need a prescription for it, so plan ahead. If your symptoms don't go away after self-treatment, see a doctor.

> Antinausea pills, such as dimenhydrinate (brand name Dramamine), are the most common over-the-counter medications used by travelers. However, side effects include drowsiness and dry mouth. For it to be effective, you must start taking it a day before your departure. If you are going on a long trip, you may want to get a prescription from your doctor for scopolamine—a thumbnail-size skin patch that you wear behind your ear.

> Pressure point bracelets help many queasy travelers. Put them on your wrists several hours before you take off. Another form of relief is taking capsules of powdered ginger (940 mg)—available at health food stores—before a trip. I also pack candied ginger and ginger snap cookies to munch en route.

> For information on inoculations and all health concerns, log on to the National Centers for Disease Control and Prevention (CDC) Web site, www.cdc.gov/travel. They also have a toll-free number, 877-FYI-TRIP (877-394-8747). The CDC will give you access to important health-related travel information, including links on vaccinations and food- and water-borne illnesses.

> Expect the worst menstrual period of your life and don't forget a pain reliever for cramps. Take along a generous supply of tampons and panty liners.

＿＿ ⅲ⅄ ＿＿

Add a pinch of salt to your Coke or Fanta or cordial: It sounds revolting but drinking it will make you feel a whole lot better. Lemon squash drink or hot lemon with sugar and salt added is also a good rehydration solution.

◆

Dr. Jane Wilson-Howarth, 46,
Shitting Pretty: How to Stay
Healthy While Traveling

➤ When traveling for extended periods of time and crossing multiple time zones, many women experience a temporary cessation of their periods. This can cause confusion about when to take birth control pills or if a pregnancy has begun. Carry the telephone number of your gynecologist back home and don't hesitate to call if you have a problem.

➤ In hot, humid climates, yeast infections are a common travel ailment. Taking antibiotics and wearing a wet bathing suit or tight pants, shorts, or panty hose can contribute to the infection. To avoid yeast infections, wear loose clothing that allows air to circulate. Cotton is better than silk or nylon. If you are prone to yeast infections, don't leave home without your medication.

➤ Long skirts with elastic waists are not only acceptable attire, they are comfortable in all types of weather. In heat, they allow air to circulate up your legs and thus reduce the incidence of yeast infections. They are also convenient when you encounter a squat toilet or when you have to go in the bushes.

➤ Be wary of swimming in tropical fresh water. Stagnant water can be home to snails carrying the tiny larvae that cause schistosomiasis, a dangerous disease that can

---

——— ⚘ ———

Getting hurt or sick while traveling may reveal fascinating aspects of the place you're visiting. On a family trip to the Philippines, I was bit by a dog. The owners of the hotel at which we were staying immediately called a local healer and before I knew it my knee was the center of a shamanic Filipino ritual involving papaya leaves, tobacco, and ancient chants. While I wouldn't recommend getting bit by an unknown animal on a remote foreign island (I did have to undergo preventive treatment for rabies upon returning to the United States), the overall experience turned out to be one of the most intriguing parts of the trip, as well as a story my family and I have told over and over.

◆

Natanya Pearlman, 29, writer/editor, San Francisco, California

damage body organs. The larvae will cause your skin to itch. Drying yourself vigorously with a towel immediately after exposure may remove most of the larvae. Before wading in, ask locals about the likelihood of such snails in the water.

➤ While it may be tempting to get an inexpensive manicure, have your ears pierced, take an acupuncture treatment, or even get a tattoo, think twice about any activities that might puncture your skin, especially in developing countries.

➤ Cold water, ice, cold cream, or toothpaste will reduce severe itching. If in the wilderness, try using mud. If you are prone to poison oak or poison ivy, always wear long pants and be prepared with special poison ivy soap.

➤ Prevent ticks and mosquito bites by using a bug spray with high DEET content. Spray your pants, socks, and all around your ankles, neck, and back.

➤ What should be in your medical kit? See the packing list in the Resources section at the end of this book.

➤ Active travelers should pack moleskin for blisters, extra socks, comfortable shoes, sunscreen, sun hats, visors, and Vaseline to apply between toes, under bra straps, and anywhere else you might experience friction while hiking.

➤ Consider taking a travel kit of basic homeopathic remedies and a homeopathic first aid book along with your standard first aid kit. Homeopathic remedies can provide rapid, inexpensive relief from such common travel ailments as digestive problems, insect bites, rashes, sore muscles, motion sickness, and many other conditions.

➤ Pack total sunblock or a very high SPF sunscreen. It can be difficult or impossible to find high-protection sunscreens overseas. Sun, wind, water, and snow reflection can damage multiple layers of skin.

➤ If you exercise regularly at home, consider jogging in the morning on your trip. Ask hotel personnel or a local person about safety and a suggestion for a scenic route. Dress modestly in loose-fitting clothes.

➤ Do not go barefoot, especially in hostel showers. This will prevent fungal and parasitic infections as well as minimize the chance of foot cuts and injuries. Always try to keep your feet clean and dry.

➤ Avoid handling animals. Even if dogs or cats seem clean and friendly, a bite from an animal while traveling could lead to a serious disease such as rabies. You don't want to ruin your trip because of an animal bite.

➤ If you are traveling for an extended period of time or to a developing country, be sure to visit your dentist prior to departure. Have your dentist look for loose fillings or unstable caps. If you are prone to dental problems, bring temporary filling material and toothache medication with you.

➤ Always carry strong pain relief pills in your cosmetic kit—but be sure to leave them in the original bottle, so customs won't ask you questions about unidentified pills.

➤ Drink plenty of bottled water to keep yourself hydrated and healthy.

➤ Wash your hands often and always carry antibacterial gel with you while you travel.

➤ When away from the comfort of your own bed, use an eye

I always pack my running shoes, and whenever I run, I'm rewarded with a sightseeing gem. I've jogged on mountain trails in Japan, around Tiananmen Square in Beijing, through a forest in Holland, and across San Francisco's Golden Gate Bridge. I always run in the morning to catch a glimpse of how locals greet the day.

♦

Alison Ashton, 33, columnist,
San Diego, California

shield, wear soft silicon earplugs, or bring your pillow with you to ensure the best rest possible.

➤ Avoid all but emergency gynecological examinations and treatment in developing countries. Inadequately sterilized instruments can spread sexually transmitted diseases.

➤ Do not take chances—always use latex condoms to reduce the risk of HIV and other sexually transmitted diseases.

➤ Women can safely scuba dive during menstruation. Don't believe the stories of menstrual blood attracting sharks. Most women use tampons, which reduce blood loss to almost nothing.

➤ The U.S. National Park Service issues leaflets that advise women not to hike in bear country during their menstrual periods. Bears do pick up human scents, but no research has proven that black or grizzly bears are specifically attracted by menstruation odors. One study suggests that polar bears, which are more carnivorous than black or grizzly bears, show the same "maximal interest" in the scent of menstrual blood as in the scent of seals, their natural prey. Whatever the real story, use caution when camping in bear country.

> Call your insurance company to verify that you have medical evacuation insurance, not just to the nearest hospital but all the way home. I was in a bus accident in Laos and I learned the hard way. After weeks in a Thai hospital, it cost me $14,000, and almost my life, to get home.
>
> ◆
>
> *Alison Wright, 38, photojournalist, San Francisco, California*

➤ If you are taking oral contraceptives, you may encounter problems if you contract traveler's diarrhea or an upset stomach. Your birth control pills may not be absorbed from your intestinal tract and you may be without protection. Doctors have recommended that if you vomit within three hours of taking a pill, take another one. After severe intestinal problems your birth control pills may not be effective. Always carry a backup method of contraception if you plan to be sexually active, and take along enough to last the entire trip. Condoms are often unavailable or of poor quality in the developing world.

➤ Motor vehicle crashes are a leading cause of injury among travelers, so walk and drive defensively. Avoid travel at night, if possible, and use seatbelts when they are available.

➤ If you do get sick and need to seek professional medical services, try to find hospitals that serve the international community in major cities overseas. Call your embassy or ask the concierge at a good hotel for a reference.

AIR TRAVEL HEALTH TIPS

➤ Staying comfortable while you fly is of the utmost importance. The temperature on airplanes can vary from tropical heat to arctic chill, and you cannot always count on having a blanket provided by the airline. Dress in layers and bring a sweater. Take everything you'll need out of your carry-on bag before you stash it overhead or under the seat in front of you.

➤ Wear loose-fitting clothes. Frequent international travelers choose comfortable slacks or long skirts so they can easily cross their legs. Do not wear tight socks or nylon knee-high stockings. If they leave a mark on your leg, then they're too tight.

➤ Place your feet on top of your carry-on bags that are stowed beneath the seat in front of you. Keep them raised off the floor to increase circulation and minimize swelling.

➤ Be conscious of your posture in the plane seat. Use the pillow offered by the airline to support your lower back. Do in-seat exercises, walk around the plane, and stretch as much as possible. Be aware of posture and movement as you get up, retrieve your carry-on bag, and deplane. This is when back injuries can occur.

➤ An inflatable travel pillow for your neck is a good investment. They are inexpensive and readily available; most international airports have luggage and accessory stores that carry them. An inflatable pillow keeps the head up and prevents pulled muscles.

➤ Avoid drinks or snacks high in sodium such as Bloody or Virgin Marys, pretzels, and peanuts. Read the labels. If you consume too much salt during a long trip, your feet may swell so much you won't be able to put your shoes back on. I've seen people walk off the plane in socks, carrying their shoes!

➤ Drink a lot of water and avoid alcohol and caffeine. Eight ounces of water per hour is recommended. Not only will this keep you hydrated, it will force you to get up and use the bathroom, thus getting you up and stretching your muscles. Carry your own water bottle aboard and ask the flight attendant to fill it often. Keep it close at hand, in the seat pocket in front of you.

➤ Use an eye shield—it will keep out the light and help you fall asleep more easily and sleep more soundly. Break it in by sleeping with it once at home prior to your trip. Adjust it so that it fits snugly over your eyes, but not so tight that you perspire. A bad fit may give you a headache and will flatten your hair! Using your eye shield is also an effective way to encourage a chatty neighbor to be quiet.

➤ Pack soft earplugs to mute airplane noise, the wailing of a baby, or the rock music seeping from your neighbor's CD player. Pellet-shaped foam earplugs will do the trick, but the soft silicone (or wax) variety that conform to the contours of your ear are the most effective.

➤ Bring cloth slippers or socks in a carry-on bag. Wear them to keep your toes warm and to let your feet breathe.

➤ Consider using melatonin or a nonprescription sleeping aid such as Excedrin PM. Many veteran travelers claim they no longer suffer from major jet lag when they use melatonin. Take melatonin for three nights after you arrive at your destination to help you adjust to the new time zone and for three nights after you return home. Check the directions on the bottle since the dosage varies.

➤ Ever wonder why you catch a cold or the flu right after a long flight? Airlines don't introduce fresh air into the cabin as often as they used to. That means you are usually breathing recycled air with everyone else's germs. Airborne diseases are easy to contract. Savvy travelers, including many pilots and airline attendants, use a tiny portable air purifier. "Air Supply" is a battery-run air purifier about the size of a pager that is worn around your neck to help remove up to 98 percent of airborne bacteria and viruses. You can find them at local travel stores or directly at www.tenex.com.

> _____ ⋇⃰⃰ _____
>
> Melatonin has changed my life. I no longer suffer from jet lag. On either end of the trip I take 2.5 milligrams of the sublingual melatonin for three nights. I finish all my pre-bed rituals—bath or shower, vitamins, eye mask on and ear plugs in, get into bed, lights out, and then I take the pill. It's miraculous.
>
> ◆
>
> *Carol Benet, Ph.D. 57, art critic, teacher, and counselor, U.C. Berkeley, Belvedere, California*

➤ Air circulated through airplane cabins is extremely dry. When traveling, carry lip balm and moisturizer in your carry-on bag to help prevent chapped lips and skin. Reapply throughout your plane ride.

➤ The effects of jet lag are generally more extreme when flying westbound. I use an all-natural homeopathic remedy called No Jet Lag, which is available at local health food stores, specialized travel stores, and markets like Magellan's and Trader Joe's.

➤ Try using different aromatherapy oils such as lavender, bergamot, neroli, or geranium, to help you relax during a long flight. To enliven a tired body after a flight, try essence of rosemary, clary sage, niaouli, or lemon.

➤ Many women experience irregular menstrual cycles because of jet lag, irregular eating and sleeping, and travel-related stress. On long flights, when long periods of sitting may aggravate pre-menstrual edema, try walking around the plane and exercising in your seat. Also consider reducing your salt intake the week before your period.

AIRPLANE STRETCHES

➤ Shoulder Shrug: Lift the top of your shoulders toward your ears until you feel mild tension in your shoulders and your neck. Hold your shoulders raised to your ears for five seconds, then relax and resume your normal posture. Do this two or three times every two hours.

➤ Back Twist: Interlace your fingers behind your head and raise your elbows straight out, parallel to the floor and level with your ears. Now pull your elbows backward and your shoulder blades toward one another. You'll feel a tension through your upper back and shoulder blades. Hold this position for ten seconds, then relax. Do it several times. This is a particularly good exercise to do when you've been sitting immobile and your shoulders and upper back are tense or tight.

➤ Head Roll: Begin with your head in a comfortable, aligned position. Slowly tilt your head to the left side to stretch the muscles on the side of your neck. Hold this stretch for ten to twenty seconds. You should feel a good, even stretch. Then tilt your head to the right side and stretch. Repeat this exercise two or three times on each side. Don't overdo it!

VI
THE GUTSY DINER

There are three items that can provide nourishment and energy for positive change: the air you breathe, the food you eat, and the ideas you ponder. Travel can literally import a breath of fresh air…. Eating new and different foods can nourish the spirit as well as the body.

—*Karen Page,* Becoming a Chef

———

MY MOST IMPORTANT DINING TIP is use common sense. Don't pass on the pastries in France, the pizza in Chicago, the *masala dosa* in India, or the food stalls in Thailand. Dining is a large part of the discovery and pleasure of travel, but it can also cause some of your worst memories.

Some people travel specifically to eat, and one of the best ways to gain an understanding of another culture is through its cuisine. The key to dining well and staying healthy is to eat the highest quality food possible. Only you can decide how bold you'll be, but it's part of the adventure of travel to try new things.

I may consider myself a risk taker, but when it comes to the equilibrium of my stomach, I am extremely cautious. Well, I did eat bamboo grubs in northern Thailand and yak eyeballs in Tibet, but both times they were well cooked and gave me less grief than eating a fast food hamburger in the USA. There are some gastronomic opportunities you just can't pass up!

When I am away from home

———

I make a deal with myself. I can try anything that I have never tasted before. I already know what chocolate, tiramisu, pâté, prime rib, smoked salmon, etc. taste like. Foods that I've never tried before and probably won't have the opportunity to sample at home are worth the exception. I give myself permission to enjoy them wholeheartedly. Everything tastes better without guilt.

◆

Laurie Armstrong, 37,
vice president, San Francisco
Convention and Visitors Bureau

for a few months, I often crave American food and atmosphere. Once, in Singapore, I treated myself to lunch in an air-conditioned restaurant in an international chain hotel. The reuben sandwich was served without sauerkraut and was both disgusting and expensive, but it satisfied a need nonetheless. I lingered to write letters for hours. It was money well spent.

Bon appétit!

TIPS

➢ Eat only thoroughly cooked food or fruits and vegetables you have peeled yourself. Remember: boil it, cook it, peel it—or forget it.

➢ Look at your meal carefully before you take the first bite. Never eat undercooked beef, pork, lamb, or poultry or raw eggs. Raw shellfish can be particularly dangerous to individuals who have liver disease or compromised immune systems.

➢ Do not eat or drink dairy products unless you know they have been pasteurized.

➢ Don't let yourself get dehydrated. Always carry a bottle of water with you when you travel and be sure to drink from it throughout the day. Do not wait for your body to tell you that you are thirsty—replenish continually.

> I relax my vegetarianism when I travel. It's much easier to make friends when I'm not trying to explain that I can't eat the foods they've kindly offered me.
>
> ◆
>
> *Jill Robinson, 33, writer, Mill Valley, California*

➢ Always carry a snack with you—you never know when you will need a little nourishment. Your growling stomach may wake you up in the middle of the night in a hotel with no room service or you could be stuck at a train station where everything is closed. Be prepared to nourish yourself immediately with nuts, dried fruit, or an energy bar.

➤ If you find yourself in a hole-in-the-wall restaurant where English is neither written nor spoken, just gesture to the waiter to follow you and walk right into the kitchen. Start pointing to this or that and make motions about how you want things cooked. The staff will love it. Ham it up. It is a great way to have a terrific meal and make friends.

Take Tabasco sauce and condiments, if the country where you are traveling is known for bland food.

◆

Michelle Fiori, 29,
administrative assistant,
advertising agency, New York

➤ When dining at food stalls, be sure the meat is well cooked or the soup has been boiling for a while. Many of my seasoned travel friends say they wouldn't miss eating the mouth-watering local specialties available, at very reasonable prices, at food stalls. Others never go near them. As for me, I size up a stall, the clientele, the vendor, the food offered, and how it is cooked. I have had many fabulous meals and only a few painful memories from food stall experiences.

➤ Take along herbal tea. In many countries there are no decaffeinated beverages available.

➤ There is protocol for eating with your hands that must be learned from the local people, as it varies from country to country. Watch how the locals eat and ask if there is a certain etiquette. For example, in Malaysia it is considered bad manners if the food touches your hand too far up your finger, past the second

Never trust a culture that doesn't value chocolate.

◆

Betsa Marsh, 48, travel writer/
photographer, Cincinnati, Ohio

knuckle. When in India, eat only using your right hand. The left hand is used for bodily hygiene and considered unclean.

➤ You will encounter different cultural challenges when dining on the road. A few you will want to remember:

Don't be surprised if you are a guest in a Muslim home and the hostess does not join you for dinner. Muslim women eat separately from the men.

If you are a guest out to dinner in Hong Kong, you can offer to pay even though it will probably not be accepted. Do not offer to split the bill, as this will result in loss of face for your host.

In Singapore, if you want to ensure good fortune, always make sure there is an even number of people present at the table.

In Taiwan, do not place your chopsticks parallel on top of your bowl or standing straight. This is bad luck and considered synonymous with a funereal ritual and death.

➤ Do not be afraid to eat by yourself in a restaurant. When choosing a restaurant, select one that appeals to your senses and mood. Do you feel like meeting other travelers? Select a lively bistro or café where you can sit at a counter or where the tables are close together. If

---

You'll always remember the lavish dinner at a highly rated, upscale restaurant at your vacation destination—if for no other reason than the price. But picnics are another way to create indelible dining memories, and they stretch your travel budget at the same time. My travels have led me to memory-making picnics. On an unusually warm spring day, my husband, Jack, and I headed for the ruins of an ancient temple and theater in Sicily. There couldn't have been a more elegant setting for our simple lunch of crusty bread, salty prosciutto, cheese, sharp olives, and sparkling mineral water. Was our picnic inconsequential when compared to the breathtaking scenery? Not at all—it was a perfect complement, giving us a chance to linger and drink more deeply of the magnificent ancient theater.

◆

Marcia Schnedler, 57, senior travel columnist, Universal Press Syndicate, Little Rock, Arkansas

you are in the mood to be alone, choose a restaurant that is quiet, where you sense you will not be bothered.

➢ If dining alone, why not ask to be seated at the counter or near the kitchen? You can pick up a number of tips while watching the staff or chef at work. Check out the growing number of restaurants that offer a counter where you can cozy up to the kitchen and personally interact with a celebrity chef.

➢ Dining alone is an acquired skill. Take a book, postcards, or stationery with you so that you can enjoy your time in the restaurant.

➢ Ask your hotel concierge about restaurants that offer communal dining. From a small table of four to a large table of thirty, you never know with whom you will be seated. It is an opportunity to connect with other people—locals and travelers.

In eight months I managed to lose thirty pounds, even while traveling to St. Louis, San Francisco, Auckland, Melbourne, and Sydney. I had a few disasters, but mostly I fared very well. At restaurants I make the server a part of my team, confiding in him that "I'm on a very low fat program (sounds better than 'diet') and I need your help." Then ask for exactly what you want: no COBS—cheese, oil, butter, or sauce. The less fuss made about your food, the better.

◆

Laurie Armstrong, 37, vice president
San Francisco Convention and Visitors Bureau

VII

ROMANCE ON THE ROAD

We travel, some of us forever, to seek other states, other lives, other souls.
—*Anaïs Nin,* The Diary of Anaïs Nin

THERE IS SOMETHING extremely romantic about travel. The change of scenery often prompts you to step outside yourself and expand your normal boundaries. Maybe at home you wouldn't talk to a strange man or woman you met in a café and then later meet them for dinner. But when traveling, general rules are often pushed aside and new adventures take place. Wonderful things can happen when you meet exotic foreigners or other travelers. Only you can decide when or if to indulge in romance on the road. You could meet the love of your life, man or woman. I met my husband in the Kathmandu Guesthouse in Nepal, and some of my friends have also met their spouses or significant others while traveling. Or they've had incredible experiences that they place very close to their heart. Keep in mind, though, that the chances of an on-the-road romance continuing once

If it hadn't been for my incurable wanderlust, I never would have met my husband. If it hadn't been for the gentle charms of the Caribbean, I'd probably still be single. It is a wonderful story with a moral most profound. Sometimes you have to listen to your heart and not your head. The very things that attracted me to Bill for a shipboard romance were what seemed to make him unsuitable as a permanent mate. China blue eyes, sun-blond hair, an over-all tan, and a nomadic lifestyle? Hardly the stuff on which to base anything long-term, I kept telling myself. Thankfully, Bill was smarter about relationships than I.

◆

Judy Wade, 50,
travel writer/photographer,
Phoenix, Arizona, in Travelers'
Tales: A Woman's World

you return home are not great. It's very difficult to keep a long-distance romance alive, but you never know when or where you'll meet your soulmate.

Although I did meet my husband in another country, I've also had experiences that haven't been as wonderful. Once, in India, I was approached by a man who was very interested in buying my Nikon camera lens. Since I didn't mind parting with it, I agreed to meet him later for coffee. The lens had simply been his way of orchestrating a meeting between us, and the minute I realized his intentions were not true—when he began to say very lascivious things to me—I made it very clear that I did not appreciate his deception or his intentions. I always encourage you to meet new people in public spaces. Be sure you know what the other person's intentions are, and also be clear about what you want out of the interaction. If you are interested in a short fling while traveling, be smart.

Gutsy Women, if you are open to love and romance on the road, always remember to be safe.

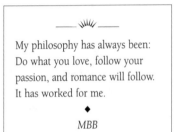
My philosophy has always been: Do what you love, follow your passion, and romance will follow. It has worked for me.

♦

MBB

TIPS

➤ If you want to meet a like-minded companion or partner, participate in an organized tour with a special focus that appeals to you, such as an archeological dig, a lesbian cruise, or an opera tour.

➤ Health spa retreats or meditation centers are good places to meet potential partners. People go to these places when they are making a life change and they are often more open and friendly. There is a time for group sharing and you talk about why you are there and what is going on in your life. Most people attend these sessions alone.

➤ Always watch your beverages while you are in a bar or

restaurant. There is a drug, rohypnol (or roofie), that may look as innocent as aspirin but is actually a very dangerous narcotic. A very potent tranquilizer similar in nature to Valium, but many times stronger, rohypnol produces a sedative effect, amnesia, muscle relaxation, and a slowing of psychomotor responses. Known as "the date-rape drug," it is very dangerous. Sedation occurs twenty-to-thirty minutes after administration and lasts for several hours.

It seems that every crewman on a Greek liner considers it part of his job to woo the passengers. The message is clear: I'll take you to paradise—as soon as I do the dishes.

◆

Betsa Marsh, 48,
travel writer/photographer,
Cincinnati, Ohio

➤ Be clear about what you want so you don't give mixed signals. If you want a fling, enjoy it. If you want something more lasting, examine your own feelings and ask yourself if his interest is genuine. Imagine introducing this person to friends and loved ones at home. Then trust your instincts.

➤ If you are the least bit inclined to find a lover, pack a supply of condoms. Remember, condoms bought in Bulgaria or India are not likely to be of the same quality as those bought at home. Many men, in many areas of the world, are not accustomed to discussing contraception and have negative feelings about using condoms, but you should insist on using them nonetheless.

➤ If you are a lesbian, you may be able to identify easily who is gay in your own culture. It is not so easy in other cultures. Try to learn the cultural attitudes toward gay people in the country you are visiting before you begin to flirt.

➤ In numerous countries, such as Pakistan, Morocco, and India, upscale hotels and tourist offices can arrange for a reliable male escort. He acts as your guide and bodyguard. This is not a cop-out.

In some Muslim areas it is worth the minimal investment to enjoy touring without continual harassment.

➤ To avoid unwanted advances, there are several things you can do:

Dress conservatively and communicate an air of confidence and respectability.

Walk with purpose.

Think and look ahead to anticipate compromising situations.

Consider wearing a wedding ring, if you don't already.

If you do have a one-night fling, be careful not to expose your money to that person. This happened to me: I got up and went to the bathroom. In the morning, after he was gone, I discovered he had stolen all the cash out of my purse. You never know who you can trust, especially if it is a guy you'll never see again.

♦

Anonymous

Try to sit or stand next to other women or family groups in restaurants, on trains or buses, and in other public places.

➤ If you begin to get pestered:

Completely ignore comments, catcalls, and whistles.

Avoid all eye contact.

Don't try to speak their language, or learn "Please leave me alone" in the local language and say forcefully.

Listen to your inner voice. If you are uncomfortable, get out of the situation immediately.

➤ If the pestering turns nasty, use forceful resistance: scream, fight, and flee! Research shows that rapists often seek to feel power and control over a weaker person. Your best defense is to resist and flee.

➤ In crowded environments like buses, men may harass you by pressing themselves against you. Don't let them get away with it. If the advance is especially ugly—suppose he presses his genitals against you—plant your elbow in his mouth, then scream at him (not swearing) in English with an air of great indignation.

➤ There is power in vocal embarrassment. I have found that many men are shamed by a verbal, loud woman admonishing them in public. Also shame them by shaking your finger in their faces. Even if the crowd doesn't understand your words, they will understand your indignation and gestures. Most sleazy men do not want public attention.

A friend told me that when she goes to work out in the fitness center of her hotel, she spends all of her time in the free-weight section. Most women gravitate to the aerobics classes and the exercise machines, so she is often the only woman in an area filled with men and there is lots of good flirting.

◆

Judith Babcock Wylie, 56, editor,
Travelers' Tales Love &
Romance, *Santa Cruz, California*

I was free and single when I was traveling so my experiences of foreign cultures were sometimes enhanced by my encounters with foreign men. I considered myself fairly sophisticated and savvy, but in retrospect I was rather naïve about my involvements—or maybe I was just hopelessly romantic. My adventures tended to obscure the reality that, as a Western woman, I've come to expect a certain level of respect and attentiveness that often wasn't granted by men of non-Western cultures. Ultimately, I realized (after many heartaches and disappointments) that I could never get what I needed from a relationship that sprang from fantasy to begin with.

◆

Kennerly Clay, 32, writer/editor, Philadelphia, Pennsylvania

VIII
BUDGET AND MONEY MATTERS

When preparing to travel, lay out all your clothes and all your money.
Then take half the clothes and twice the money.

—*Susan Heller*

———

ALTHOUGH I HAVE BEEN ASKED dozens of times what it cost me
to travel around the world for a year, it is almost impossible for me
to say what it will cost you to stay for a month in Asia or two weeks
in Europe. What you will spend depends on where you stay, where
and what you eat, how you travel (plane, train, bus, rental car, on
foot or bike), and how fast you travel. One person who travels twice
as fast as another will spend a great deal more. Transportation, trans-
fers in and out of cities, and lodging are a large percentage of a budget. A week lying on the beach in southern Thailand watching the
waves roll in brings down your daily costs. If you stay in luxury
hotels, fly everywhere, or see a lot of countries in a very short time
you can spend a lot of money.

I spent under $4,000 to travel for a year, spending most of that
time in Southeast Asia. That included all of my airfare, food, gifts,
communications home—everything. Perhaps I could have spent half
this amount, but I didn't want to scrimp and stay in dormitories or
the cheapest hotels, always travel second class on trains, and learn to
exist on rice and tea. I splurged to fly to Sri Lanka and the Maldives
(where I went scuba diving...talk about expensive), and I enjoyed
the old-fashioned Raj-style luxury of India's charming Maharaja
Palace hotels. Remember that, most times, you will get what you pay
for and many times its worth in unique experiences by paying a little more.

If you are traveling independently and are not going to one location (such as a condo in Hawaii), the best way to figure out a budget

for yourself is to buy a good guidebook and study it. Spend some time in a specialized travel bookstore sifting through the guides available for your destination. You can learn a great deal about the average prices for lodging, food, transportation, and entertainment in this way.

Unless you have a generous budget for your travels, choose your activities and countries carefully. Many areas of Asia (Nepal, India, Indonesia, Thailand, parts of China) and South America (Peru, Ecuador) are not only inexpensive areas to travel, they are also very welcoming to women. The longer you are gone from home, the lower your per diem will be. If you have the time, plan on staying in one area for a week or more. You will

My well-kept secret for taking a very inexpensive getaway trip is to go somewhere, by myself or with a friend, and stay in a hostel. They have kitchens and dining rooms and common rooms. In the evenings there is a great mix of people from around the world. Most of them are under thirty, but there are some "boomers" and "seniors." You basically walk into an instant dinner party with interesting international guests.

♦

Cathy Beaham, 36, marketing consultant, Kansas City, Missouri

meet more local people as well as experienced travelers and learn where to eat, what to do, and where to stay. When I traveled around the world I focused on remote areas where I knew I could not go on a short corporate vacation. I discovered that the longer I was gone, the less I spent.

TIPS

➤ Budget killers include not shopping around for your plane tickets; calling home too often; using taxis excessively; eating out all the time; staying at international chain hotels. When in doubt, ask other travelers (before and during your trip) for their budget, lodging, and restaurant tips.

➤ You can save a lot of money by planning in advance. Consider alternative accommodations. For example, if you have done your research about Ireland, you will have learned about all the bed-and-breakfasts in the country. Not only are they much less expensive than staying in a hotel, they offer a huge breakfast, warm hospitality, and a chance to meet the people, not just see the sights. I have stayed in bed-and-breakfasts in the USA (even in Los Angeles!) to cut costs and add charm and intimacy to my travels.

You'll go broke if you don't do your own laundry most of the time, especially in Europe. If the radiator is running, you're in luck. Just make sure you stand by and flip the clothes often, or they'll overcook. Use wooden hangers for drying the dark colors, or you'll end up with stains.

◆

Joan Medhurst, 49, retired professor, Alameda, California

➤ Vary your travel. Try second class some of the time. Cut your transportation costs by traveling the way locals do.

➤ Ask the locals where they eat out. Leave the tourist areas of a city to find less expensive restaurants in more residential neighborhoods.

➤ Don't buy a whole new wardrobe for your trip prior to departure. Keep your pre-trip shopping to a minimum. Buy what you need as you travel.

➤ Negotiate the price of your hotel room. If you've got the guts, why not try? You must call the hotel directly; do not use the central 800 number.

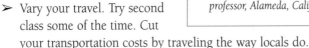

I don't have a great deal of money to travel, so I rent my house and then go to developing countries where I can live for much less than my house rental.

◆

Virginia Barton Brownback, 72, writer/photographer, Inverness, California

Decide how much you can spend, wait until late in the day, and speak to the hotel manager. Tell him what you can spend. Hotel rooms are a perishable item. Often they will accommodate you. Your chances of getting a lower rate for a room are better on the weekend in the city and during the week in the country.

➤ When making reservations for car rental, accommodations, or miscellaneous tickets, always mention your membership in an organization—the American Association of Retired Persons (AARP), AAA—or affiliation to an academic institution. Often discounts are available for the asking.

➤ For airline tickets, car rentals, and hotel rooms, always ask, "Is this the lowest rate available today?"

➤ If you are staying at an establishment for a long time, or will be returning often, meet with the management and negotiate a special rate.

➤ Travel with a pocket calculator. I use it to help me figure out the exchange rate until I've worked out a simple formula. I use it to calculate the approximate amount of a credit card charge (in U.S. dollars), which I write at the bottom of each receipt.

➤ Make a double-sided photocopy of your credit cards, travelers checks, ATM card, passport, and eyeglass or contact lens prescription to carry in your money belt.

_____ ⋇ _____

Keep $20 in small bills tucked away at all times. You may be leaving a country and find out there is a departure tax or if you need a tip upon arriving in a new country. This will save you from having to stand in line to get local currency at inconvenient and often stressful departure and arrival times.

◆

MBB

➤ Play purchasing exercises with yourself while window-shopping to build your sense of the local currency—when you are ready to step into the store or stall, you will be better prepared to bargain. Memorize a currency "ladder" if you find it helps, e.g., how many rupees constitute $5, $10, $50? If you have a spending limit for a certain item, keep that number in mind in the foreign currency, not just in dollars.

➢ Protect your valuables. All of your important documents and money should be worn on your body. Buy a comfortable money belt or neck pouch. When the shoeshine boy and his buddies robbed a friend in Rio, they snatched the bills he took out of his trouser pocket and ran. They got $14. He had another $50 inside his sock and clothing. Only pull out small amounts of money at a time.

➢ Consider staying in a youth hostel. They are safe, friendly, people-oriented places filled with other budget-minded, adventurous travelers. There are over 5,000 hostels in 70 countries, including 150 in the USA. Not only do hostels offer extensive information about what to do locally, you will meet people who have already been where you may want to go and can give you the inside scoop on the good places to see, eat, and shop. Some hostels offer bicycle, canoe, or kayak rentals. Hostels typically cost from $12 to $22 a night.

———— ☼ ————

Every year since 1979, my friend Renae and I have left husband (hers), children (hers and mine), and, most recently, our grandchildren at home for destinations overseas. This past spring, our plans were to see how inexpensively we could travel in England and Scotland and at the same time do everything that excites us: go to the theater, see old friends, find the finest gardens, visit museums and art galleries. We wondered, as well, just how flexible and adaptable we really were, how well we'd cope with the unknown. So both of us decided that nothing less than staying at youth hostels would do. On the cheap, we concurred, is not just for the young! Would we do it again? Yes!

◆

Rachel Pollack, 60, author and travel writer, Denver, Colorado

➢ Courier travel is an option that is neither dangerous nor illegal. Some shipping companies need to transport documents from one country to another quickly, so they ask a courier to fly to a destination with little or no checked baggage. The shipping company sends a representative to the airports of departure and arrival to handle the details of the company's checked luggage. Couriers do not fly for free—their airfare is subsidized. You must be at least eighteen years old.

➤ These days YMCAs aren't just for young Christian men! There are branches in many major cities throughout the world, such as Hong Kong and New Delhi, that are safe and well located. You can make a reservation with a phone call and a credit card. If you don't like the accommodations or location, you can move after the first night. Be careful that the facility is not located in an unsafe neighborhood.

➤ If you travel in and out of major cities, use ATM withdrawals and credit card advances. If you'll be in remote areas for long periods of time, consider traveler's checks and some cash.

➤ The best exchange rate you will find is through ATMs because they provide local currency (debiting your bank account at home). They give you the wholesale exchange rate and this can be from 5 to 10 percent higher than you get at hotels or exchange offices! Check with your bank about how to access your account overseas.

➤ When traveling internationally, it is recommended that your credit or debit PIN be four digits long. If your PIN is longer than four digits, consider contacting your financial institution and ask them to issue you a new PIN number. If you have an alphabetic PIN, translate the letters into numbers before leaving the country.

When traveling to developing countries, make sure that your bills are crisp and clean. Twice, once in Africa and once in Asia, banks refused to take my large bills because they had ink marks and they were dirty. Many shopkeepers will also refuse soiled or marked bills.

◆

MBB

➤ Guard your PINs carefully, whether they are for your ATM card or your telephone credit card. Stand close to the phone when dialing and punching in your number. Phone card thieves work public places with binoculars.

➤ Financial institutions may have restrictions on daily withdrawals that apply even when you are in another country. Check with your bank to find out how much you can take out each day.

➤ Before returning to the USA, convert all of your foreign coins and bills into U.S. dollars at the airport. Banks and exchange offices in the U.S. only accept bills and charge a hefty fee. Last summer I returned from Canada with $10 in Canadian bills. The fee to convert them to U.S. currency was $5. If you plan to return to that country again soon, you may be better off just holding on to the currency.

I have a long necklace made of carved, wooden, children's toy animals, strung on a simple bright string. It is the only piece of jewelry I have taken on trips for a decade, and I wear it day and night when away. Invariably, it provokes curiosity, makes me seem friendlier and not so scary, and prompts people to touch the little toys, to begin to talk about these charming little carvings (in whatever language), and finally to smile. A barrier broken. All over the world, my magic necklace draws children like a magnet. Their parents follow. Even if you don't take photos, but just want to make contact, as I often do, with those beautiful people around the world who aren't found at the tourist beaches or bars, you can find something similar to provoke a smile, a moment of curiosity—an opening. And that opening is what transforms you from an outsider or an intruder into a friend.

◆

Paula McDonald, 50+, author and photojournalist, Baja California, Mexico

IX
BARGAINING AND TIPPING

Bargaining is a game around the world—a game of wit and skill and words. Bring your best poker face, and prepare for fearless entertainment.

—*Kathy Borrus,* The Fearless Shopper

I LOVE TO WANDER through bazaars and markets looking for local handicrafts when traveling. I use different negotiating styles with different vendors, rickshaw drivers, or cabbies and in different situations. Some travelers find bargaining humiliating, while others revel in it. It can be an unexpected source of local information and even friendship. When I find haggling with street vendors degrading, I give in or don't buy. I am rarely on a budget so tight that I can't spend an extra dollar or two.

Once I fell in love with a beautiful jade disk necklace in the old town in Hanoi. I saw it in the glass cases of several shops before I asked the price and began to compare the workmanship on the hand-tooled silver casing. When I finally found a shop with several nice ones, I began to bargain. From the very beginning, I should have realized I had met my match, laughed, and given up. But I didn't. The Vietnamese woman, about my age, grew tired of my negotiating. She

In the United States, you're a person as much as you are a woman; in most of the world, you learn that you are only a woman—until you pull out your credit card.

♦

Joan Medhurst, 49, retired professor, Alameda, California

appealed to my husband and to our guide, and finally, with an air of indignation after my last offer, she bellowed, "Lady you cheap!" It is a funny story to tell now but, at the time, I was humiliated. I paid her asking price and hurried off. In the end, we were both losers, because I was planning to buy three necklaces instead of one. I smile and think of her every time I wear my "Lady You Cheap" necklace. She taught me an important lesson—pay the higher price and get what you want.

A friend of mine once bargained for a set of silver pony bells in a Tibetan town, but the old man offering them was absolutely unyielding in his price: $50 U.S. This seemed very high given the other goods and prices being offered at the market, and so my friend went home without the bells. Eight years later he reports that every Christmas he thinks wistfully of those bells as he puts up decorations. He realized that the bells may well have had a history for the old man, who was reluctant to part with them unless he got a very good price. Remember that the worth of something lies not in what is paid for the item, but what it means in your heart and life.

BARGAINING TIPS

➢ Before you begin bargaining, decide if you really want to buy the item. Do not waste your time or the salesperson's.

➢ Decide the top price you are willing to pay and know what that amount is in the local currency. Travel with a pocket calculator and use it to figure out the exchange rate before you pass through the doors of temptation.

➢ Eye contact with a shopkeeper will lead to a conversation. If you look them in the eyes, it can lead to a string of questions and it may be difficult to extricate yourself from the conversation without feeling rude.

➢ Do not be taken in by engaging come-ons, such as this summons by a leather merchant in Antalya, Turkey, "Madame, I have everything you want." Shopkeepers can be humorous and talented manipulators and will play on your sense of politeness. Only enter stores that you want to, and walk by those that you do not wish to enter—no matter how much the salesperson chides you.

➢ Occasionally accept offers of hospitality. I sipped a hot cup of apple tea in a spice market in Marmaris, Turkey, and heard all about a merchant's family and spice business. I did purchase spices from him, and even if I overpaid a little, it was worth it because I have the memory of the time spent with him in his booth.

➤ Don't ask the price right away. In fact, look disinterested in the item you would like to buy. When you ask the price, if it is above what you had decided you would pay for such an item, leave. After this tactic, the merchant will usually approach you with a better price. Let the bargaining begin!

➤ Don't rush a good negotiation. Chat and have fun with it. Remember, it's all a dance and you will know when you are comfortable buying the item or walking away.

Many people will ask you for money. Try to avoid giving money, especially to beggars on the street. In developing countries, they are often professionals. Be careful whom you give to. Not only will you burn out if you are cheated, but you may turn proud people into beggars. You will often know when people really need it.

◆

Olga Murray, 71, president, Nepal Youth Opportunity Foundation, Sausalito, California

➤ Bargaining will vary from country to country. In India, for example, the first counteroffer can be 40 percent of the asking price and hopefully you can meet in the middle. In Turkey, however, you may only bargain for a ten or fifteen percent reduction. Ask the hotel manager, taxi driver, tour guide, or a local what they consider the local bargaining rules to be.

➤ Communicate shipping and payment arrangements early in the negotiations. If you are paying by credit card, the price may be higher. If you pay in cash, see what kind of discount this will add. If shipping an item, make sure that you agree upon shipping method and time frame.

➤ If you are interested in buying more than one item, use that information as a bargaining tool for a larger discount.

➢ If you can afford the item, don't haggle over pennies or even dollars. Consider the merchant's lifestyle. The extra income could make a big difference in his or her life—if it won't impact your own, then pay a little more.

➢ Enjoy your new purchase and the relationship you made with the merchant. Don't look at the price of the same item later in the market, as it may only upset you. Be happy with the item and the experience.

➢ Even if you end up not purchasing an item you have been bargaining for, be pleasant and leave the merchant on good terms.

I remember negotiating with a boat family in Halong Bay in Vietnam who lived aboard their twelve-foot wooden skiff. They had no sewage facilities, no running water, and only a tarp to cover them in the rainy season. Two years after our encounter I still regret that I haggled over the price of fresh crab. In retrospect, I should have paid the full asking price. It wasn't much. The extra income would have made a big difference in their lives. When in doubt, pay the asking price.

◆

MBB

➢ Contrary to popular wisdom, duty-free shops are not always filled with bargains. International passengers do not have to pay local taxes since they are exiting the country with the items, but sometimes merchants mark up prices to take advantage of a captive audience. If you have done your research and know what you are looking for, then there are bargains to be had.

TIPPING TIPS

➢ There is no worldwide standard for tipping for services, but here is my rule of thumb: Never tip less than the price of a beer in the local currency.

➢ What might be viewed as a discretionary tip in our culture may be a necessary bribe for basic services in another. For example, in India tipping is a way of getting things accomplished. I have discovered that in some countries you must tip restroom attendants to receive a paper towel or toilet paper. If you don't tip them, they may follow you with a stream of insults.

➤ In addition to giving a monetary tip to someone like your guide, with whom you have spent several days, add something that will be meaningful to him or her. After climbing Mount Kilimanjaro, my husband and I tipped our guide in cash and gave him our daypack. He was absolutely overjoyed with it because such packs were unavailable in Tanzania.

If you don't bargain, what is the worst thing that can happen? You might pay a little more than you would have if you'd haggled; a merchant in a developing country you don't know will gloat over hoodwinking a naïve tourist—but you'll end up with the object you wanted to have and maintain a mood you also wanted to keep.

◆

Claire Walter, editor/travel writer, Boulder, Colorado

➤ If a taxi does not have a working meter, or the driver won't use one, avoid hassles or misunderstandings at the end of your taxi journey by negotiating the fare prior to entering the cab. Have a piece of paper available and insist he write the amount on it. Then be prepared for him to make one last effort for more money before you get out.

➤ In some cultures tipping is not customary or recommended. In Singapore it is officially discouraged and in Japan it is virtually unknown. In other cultures the service charge or gratuity is included in every bill. Ask a local person about the tipping customs of the country you are visiting.

➤ If tips are automatically included in a bill it is not necessary to leave more, but it may be customary to leave a small amount in cash. For example, in good Parisian restaurants the French leave an additional 5 percent on the table.

➤ Be careful when you sign your credit card charge form. Most receipts have a separate box for the gratuity. If there is no tip box on the form, ask the waiter how to include it in the charge.

➤ Some unscrupulous restaurant personnel have been known to write the total amount of the bill, including a predetermined tip and service charge, in the top box of the charge slip. They leave the "tip" and "total" boxes empty and fill in an additional tip and new total after you have signed the bill. Ask if the tip is included and if it is, rewrite the total at the bottom before signing.

➤ Make sure to thank flight attendants who give you good service. They have a tough job and aren't paid well these days, nor are they allowed to accept tips. But a smile and a "thank you" can mean a lot.

✕
COMFORT ON THE ROAD

Up in the air you breathed easily, drawing in a vital assurance and light-
ness of heart. In the highlands you woke up in the morning and thought:
Here I am, where I ought to be.

—*Isak Dinesen,* Out of Africa

WHEN I'M TRAVELING, there are always little things I do to remind
myself of home. I have heard numerous stories of the various ways
women create rituals to help them relax or find a little bit of home
on the road. Whether you are stressed out because of transportation
hassles—airline delays, cancelled flights, missed trains—or you need
a way to get back in touch with yourself when you are feeling swept
away, rituals are simply something that you do to feel comfortable
and more in control.

When you travel, there are many times when you may need a ritual to reduce stress and clear a way for you to enjoy your destination.
Maybe you are on a business trip and you simply need to do something that will make you feel like you have a life outside of work. The
following rituals are small things you can do to retreat from your
travel life and focus on yourself.

I'm sure if you begin to think about it, you will realize that you
do have a few rituals that you practice on the road. I encourage you
to consider the following and invent your own. It's important to take
care of yourself while you travel. Next time you travel and are feeling
frustrated or overwhelmed, breathe deeply and try one of the following exercises.

RITUALS

➤ Sit still and listen to your breath.

➤ Put on comfortable clothes and stretch. Start with your neck
   and work your way through your whole body.

➤ Light a candle and meditate. Focus on your breath and empty your mind of all of the thoughts that are racing around. This will enhance your pleasure of what's to come.

➤ Take a long bath. Bring bubble bath and candles from home to make it special. If you don't have any accessories, simply relax in a warm tub.

➤ Listen to music.

➤ Take a shower and stand still for a minute to feel the warm water trickling from your head down to your toes. Imagine your discomfort and tension being washed away, leaving you cleansed and refreshed.

_____ ⚜ _____

While traveling, I set aside time each day to write in my journal. What are five new things I saw today? Whom did I meet? How do I feel? It slows me down to notice the details of my journey, so I can savor the people, the sights, the food, my inner landscape. It helps me realize that my travels are not just about viewing the world, they're about truly seeing myself.

◆

Lisa Bach, 31, editor,
Oakland, California

➤ Leave your lodging and find somewhere outdoors to sit. Wander through a park, watch the locals from afar, or stare at the moon. Just be still and let the world pass around you.

➤ Practice reflexology. Give your ear a massage and it will be like you had a full body message. There are over a hundred reflexology energy points located in your ears that are connected to different organs and body parts.

➤ Wake up the Chinese way. Practice tai chi, an ancient martial art form. If you are lucky enough to be in Hong Kong, contact the Hong Kong Tourist Association for free lessons—in English—three mornings a week in the Garden Plaza, Hong Kong Park (800-282-4582).

➤ Read a good book. Bring along a couple of paperbacks to read along the way. When you finish one, exchange it with another traveler.

➤ Keep a journal while you travel. This way, as your outer journey advances, you will advance inwardly as well. Also consider writing down five things you are grateful for each day. This may be as simple as calling home and hearing your daughter's voice or the Belgian waffle that you had on an afternoon walk through Bruges.

➤ Carry a reporter's notebook for scribbling down notes along your journey—train schedules, favorite restaurants that you stumbled across, names and addresses of people you meet, impressions of the sights and towns you visit. You never know when you will need this information. You might use it to pass along tips to other travelers or when you return home and want to write a story or letter about your trip.

➤ Make a scrapbook as you travel. All the ticket stubs, brochures, maps, and other things you pick up in your travels make ideal material for your scrapbook. If you take a scrapbook, a pair of scissors, and a glue stick with you on your trip, the ten minutes you spend each night on your scrapbook will make it a treasured item. Otherwise, you might end up with a bag of miscellaneous items that never make it into a book because you are not quite sure what they are or where you collected them.

MAKE YOUR HOTEL ROOM
A HOME AWAY FROM HOME

So many people complain about their hotel rooms—why not make improvements to them instead? Even if you are only staying for a couple of nights, try to make it feel as much like home as possible.

➤ Unpack your suitcases and put them away. Do not live out of the suitcases. If you are used to having a sock and underwear drawer, then unpack and create the same organization.

➤ Place a framed photo of your family or friends on the bedside table.

➤ If you are used to having flowers in your home, go to a local florist and get yourself a small bouquet to keep in your room. Or keep the flower from a room-service cart for your room.

➤ Move the desk to where it is most comfortable for you to work. If you like to have a view or more natural sunlight when you read or write, move the desk near the window.

➤ When you buy presents for friends and family, have them gift-wrapped with a pretty ribbon. Leave these gifts out in your hotel room for a festive look and a connection to home.

➤ Hide all of the hotel's promotional reading material and place your magazines or books in their place.

XI
THE BUSINESS TRAVELER

Enjoy the place you are visiting. Don't work all the time.
—*Anonymous Frequent Flyer*

GUTSY BUSINESSWOMEN—we're everywhere: on airplanes, checking into hotels, renting cars, giving speeches, talking on cell phones, and making important deals all over the world. Business travel is an essential part of modern corporate life, and in the next few years over 50 percent of all business travelers will be women.

Travel is a wonderful perk for many working women, although after the first few trips many individuals do not find it fun or glamorous anymore. It adds stress and consumes personal time we might rather spend with friends and family. Can we learn ways to be smart business travelers? Frequent flyers whose jobs demand that they travel will tell you "Yes." They live on airplanes, at airports, in hotels, driving countless miles in rental cars.

Here are some basic, road-tested tips to help make your business travel easier.

Room service? The part I love is that it's perfectly decadent. I stay in, order anything I want from room service, lounge around in my nightgown, forget my table manners, take a bath, watch trash on TV. Of course, being decadent is only enjoyable for about one night in any city.

Laurie Armstrong, 37, vice president, San Francisco Convention and Visitors Bureau

TIPS

➢ Record all of your confirmation numbers—hotel, car rental, flight information, etc.—in your calendar, Palm Pilot, or journal. I have jotted down these vital numbers on my airline ticket jacket and later discovered that an efficient ticket agent threw it away and gave me a clean one. If your reservation is lost or the computer is down, you will be prepared. If your flights are delayed, you'll need to call ahead to confirm a late arrival; if you bring the vital phone and confirmation numbers with you, handling the situation will be a breeze.

> Pack lightly, bringing only carry-on luggage if possible. Pack the least amount of clothes you think you can survive on. You can wear the same mix-and-match outfits day after day. Leave room in your bag for shopping treasures you can't resist along the way.

> How many shoes does the gutsy business traveler pack? Too many, usually! If the shoe fits, wear it, don't carry it. Wear the shoes you'll need for business and pack one pair of athletic shoes for walking, jogging, or informal occasions.

> Pack dark clothes. They don't show spots or dirt and work for most situations.

> If you need to be dressed in business attire at your meeting, be sure to wear it on the plane or carry it with you; if your luggage is delayed or lost, you won't be forced to shop.

> Sleep smart. Dark circles under your eyes aren't good for business. Carry eye shields and earplugs to counter jet lag or a poor night's sleep in a strange hotel room. Silicone earplugs work

I have a cosmetic bag prepacked with travel size items that I know I always need when I'm traveling for business. I never have to worry about getting somewhere and not having a toothbrush, toothpaste, shampoo, conditioner, Q-tips, deodorant, etc. It's a great relief to simply grab the kit and go.

◆

Kim Arnone, 32, attorney,
Berkeley, California

best, muting noise, snoring, and annoying chatty airline neighbors. Also, invest in a blow-up pillow to help you sleep soundly on the plane—it will also prevent your hair from being flattened as you sleep, and your neck from getting a crick.

➤ Ask for a hotel room away from the ice machine, elevator, and on the quiet side of the building. It can make a huge difference for your sleep that night and your mood the next day.

➤ Hotel alarm clocks and wake-up services can be unreliable. Pack an inexpensive sports watch with an alarm. Use the stop-watch to time international phone calls as a reminder to keep them short.

➤ Carry C rations. Airlines offer little more than the tiny, salty servings of peanuts or pretzels for short flights. If your flight is delayed or has mechanical problems, you may spend hours on the runway or circling in the air while your stomach is screaming. Carry a nutritious and filling power bar and an apple in your briefcase.

➤ Before driving off the lot at the rental car agency, walk around the vehicle to check for dents or other damage. Insist that everything be verified in writing by the rental agent and keep a copy.

➤ If you must leave valuables or luggage in your vehicle, be sure they are locked in the trunk or well hidden.

> Befriend the bellboys for the most reliable information about the safety of walking from your hotel to a nearby pharmacy, restaurant, or meeting place. They are the best source of information about the neighborhood. Don't hesitate to ask them to walk you there.

♦

Alice Bond, 48, business executive, Coral Springs, Florida

➤ Pack more than double the number of business cards you think you will need. Handing someone your card makes a professional statement and immediately establishes your credibility.

➤ Have your business information printed on the reverse side of your cards in the language of the country where you will be doing business.

➤ If you are doing business in Asia, present your business card with both hands. After you accept your colleague's card, carefully and respectfully store it in a good place. Don't just slip it into your back pocket.

➤ The concierge at your international hotel is your best source of local information and help.

➤ How much money do you need? With a bank card or major credit card, you can obtain cash in almost every major city in the world. If you are prone to forgetting your PIN number at home, then write down a coded version in the back of your passport.

> _\\\\////_

In Asia, introductions are an important part of the business ritual. When a business colleague presents his or her card, take a moment to read it through and then keep it in view during your discussion as a show of respect.

◆

Linda C. Adams, 40+,
travel marketing consultant,
Laguna Niguel, California

➤ Calling card thieves try to steal your long-distance calling card number by looking over your shoulder in large airports, bus terminals, and train stations. Make a habit of blocking the phone buttons with your free hand or a piece of paper before you punch in your code.

➤ Laptop computers have become a popular item for theft. Stay on the alert, especially when passing through security X-ray machines. A thief watches you place your laptop on the conveyer belt of the X-ray machine, then cuts in line in front of you and sets off the metal detector. While you are delayed, your laptop passes through the machine and a second thief snatches it and quickly disappears. Another technique involves someone spilling coffee or ketchup on you. When you stop and put down your bags to clean it off, be sure your laptop is secured firmly between your legs.

➤ If you will be making several credit card calls from your hotel room, don't hang up between calls, or you will be charged a fee for each call. Most hotel phone systems will allow you to hit the # key for a new dial tone between calls and you will avoid additional charges.

➤ Mix pleasure with your business. When your time is limited, a tour can help you see the best of what the city has to offer and can be a great way to treat a client.

SMART AND SAFE

➤ Business women on the road have safety concerns that men don't. Be smart and safe in your business travels.

➤ Look and act confident. Get directions ahead of time and know your destination. If you are unsure of your location, act like you know where you are headed and get directions at a safe-looking gas station, café, or market.

➤ Be aware of your surroundings (people, cars, doorways, stairwells) and have a plan in case you get into a dangerous situation. Be prepared to act quickly, scream for help, kick, and run.

➤ Be proactive, not reactive.

➤ Never volunteer that you are traveling alone. Lie if necessary.

➤ Know where you're going before setting out in a rental car.

➤ Do not reveal a map in your car with a marked route on it.

➤ To ward off unwanted male attention, especially in male-dominated foreign countries, carry fake engagement and wedding rings to be used as necessary; make hotel reservations as if married.

➤ Write your first initial and last name on your luggage tags to conceal your gender. Or use laminated business cards as luggage tags so that strangers do not know your home address.

➤ Carry your passport, plane ticket, traveler's checks, and cash in a concealed money belt worn under your clothes.

➤ When alone (particularly at night), walk with the crowd and act as if you're part of the pack.

➤ If you will be arriving at night, rental car companies and hotels can arrange for someone to accompany you to and from parking lots.

➤ For peace of mind when traveling alone, choose national hotel chains with interior room entrances, as opposed to motel-style outside entrances. More and more women are also choosing small inns and bed-and-breakfasts where the proprietors are more aware of their activities and will become alarmed if they don't return by a specific time.

➤ When first arriving in your room, hold the door open with your luggage while you check the closets. If you're alone and feel unsafe, ask someone from the front desk to accompany you while you check out your room.

➤ When staying in hotels, always check the window and door locks.

➤ If your hotel room has a sliding door to the outside, make sure it is locked.

➤ Always keep your hotel room door locked. If someone knocks and there's a peephole, look to see who's there. If the person identifies himself as a hotel employee, ask him to come back later, or call the front desk to verify his identity and purpose for coming to your room.

➤ Place the "Do Not Disturb" sign on your door or leave the TV or radio on to discourage anyone from entering your room while you are away.

➤ Keep the curtains in your room closed if your room is located on the first floor or looks out onto a walkway.

➤ If the desk clerk mentions your room number out loud and there are other guests who can overhear, request that you be given a different room and that the clerk not mention the number.

➤ When you're using room service order forms, don't indicate that you're alone or use your first name (which can identify you as a woman). Or skip the forms entirely and order your breakfast over the telephone.

Before I pack my jewelry, whether it is expensive (or expensive looking), I ask myself if it will fit in or if it will be appropriate in a business setting. In Paris, probably; in Quito, probably not. In some cities, wearing expensive jewelry is an invitation to mugging. Consider the context of where you are going and what you will be doing.

MBB

XII

First-Time Travelers and Gutsy Graduates

*If I had my life to live over again, I'd try to make more mistakes next time.
I would relax. I would limber up. I would be sillier than I have been. I
would take more chances. I would take more trips. I would climb more
mountains, swim more rivers, and watch more sunsets.*

—Nadine Stair, "I'd Pick More Daisies"

ALL OVER THE COUNTRY, women of all ages have asked me to give them some words of encouragement to help them step out the door. Some ask, "Do you think I should go?" I tell them "Yes." To boost my self-confidence before I took off on my journey around the world, this is what I did: Every morning as I looked into my mirror, I asked myself, *What's holding you back? What is the worst that could happen? How will you feel about yourself in six months or a year if you don't fulfill your dream? Look at everything you have already accomplished. This is just one more little risk. You know that the first step is the hardest. So quit agonizing over the decision and just go!*

I tell all young people: Travel now while your knees are good and before you settle down. People put off travel for many reasons, but you should do it while you are mobile, active, interested in meeting and learning about people.

◆

Rosemary Gardner, 79, retired social worker, Oakland, California

TIPS

➤ Before you go, decide honestly what the most important goals are for your trip. Do you want to see lots of sights? Meet as many people as possible? Get to know yourself better? Begin learning a new language? You will be tempted by many choices, but having a clear idea in mind of what you really want from your journey will help you decide what to do and what to skip and you will return home feeling satisfied.

➤ Make a conscious decision about your preferred travel companions. Think through your goals and what you are willing to compromise. Do your homework. Call numerous tour operators, collect and read brochures, read guidebooks, then consider traveling with a like-minded group or alone. One of your most important decisions will be who you travel with. Don't make this decision hastily.

➤ If you choose to travel independently, consider arranging a homestay at the beginning of your trip. It can be as simple as renting a room with a family or arranging an extended stay at a family guesthouse. See the Resources section for a list of organizations that arrange homestays.

➤ Bring one totally impractical thing that makes you feel at home. Travel with your own pillow or favorite well-worn book. Throw in a skirt that helps you feel refreshed and energized after wearing the same clothes over and over again.

➤ Make sure your baggage is properly routed at check-in. It is very easy for a tired airline employee to misroute a bag with the wrong destination tag. Learn the particular code for your destination.

➤ If your seatmate on an airplane, bus, or train is driving you nuts with non-

We all share a desire to fulfill our dreams, but few of us act on it. Over and over again women tell me that taking an adventure travel vacation was often the first time they acted on a totally new experience in their lives. For the first time they went somewhere alone, met new people, or learned about another culture. For the first time they experienced an active vacation and physically challenged themselves. They have all come away feeling a newfound and positive sense of self.

♦

Susan Eckert, 50, founder and president, Adventure Women, Bozeman, Montana

stop talk, put on headphones, if you have them, smile, and turn your head away.

➤ In many developing countries you will be hassled by men in airport terminals who offer cheap transportation into town. Don't accept their offers. Seek out a ground transportation desk near the baggage claim area for assistance.

➤ Create cheat sheets for local lingo. It is important to be able to say a few rudimentary words in the local language, such as *please, thank you, beautiful, spicy, not spicy,* and *delicious.* To cheat easily and help you memorize the vocabulary, write basic words on a small sheet of paper for reference.

➤ When you first arrive in a new city, if you can, take a half-day tour to get oriented.

➤ Before heading out to explore a new city, pick up a business card from your hotel. It's easier than you think to get lost and forget your way back, and a card in your possession will tell taxi drivers or anyone you ask for directions where you want to go. This is particularly important in countries like Thailand, Japan, or China, where you may not be able to read the script and locals may not speak or read English.

➤ Establish routines. Connect to the place you're visiting by going to the same coffee shop every morning and reading the paper. Stroll along the river, waterfront, or town square each evening and you'll start to see familiar faces. It can help you feel a sense of belonging in a new location.

➤ Whether traveling by bus, train, plane, or boat, try to sit next to another woman if you want to avoid potential come-ons. You may well make a new friend.

➤ Consider leaving your purse at home and using a small fanny pack, worn around your waist, to carry bills and coins, a hairbrush, lipstick, and other small items. Wear it in front, not behind, which would make it a temptation to pickpockets.

➤ Also carry a small or medium-size backpack for all the things you'll need during the day: journal, camera, film, water bottle, sweater, guidebook. Select one with a sturdy zipper, several compartments, and padded shoulder straps. Keep the backpack secure with a combination lock.

➤ Last-minute purchases in the airport that make a difference: a pack of gum to relieve pressure in your ears, if needed, and for bad breath; postcards of your hometown to share or give away; snacks to stave off midnight hunger while you are adjusting to new mealtimes.

GUTSY GRADS TIPS

➤ Savor the moment. You've worked hard, and this is your chance to learn about the world in a hands-on way. Fully enjoy yourself and the wonders of the road.

➤ Stay in touch! Calm your concerned mom (or dad, grandmother, friend)—call home.

➤ Are you traveling with friends? Spend part of the day on your own and meet up for dinner. That way, you'll get important time to yourself, have your own stories to tell, and remain appreciative of each others' company.

➤ Don't push your limits where there are no safety

I once talked a friend into hiking through a Malaysian jungle, a nine-day adventure that we decided to do on our own and without the mandatory guide. After all, we were on a budget and $500 for a guide seemed a bit too steep. It was the start of monsoon season and one night, while camping next to a big river, we were caught in a flash flood. Our boots, stove, and dishes were swept away by the thundering torrent and we had to walk back to park headquarters three days and thirty miles away—barefoot! I've learned that there's a fine line between risk and reward, and that not all rules are made to be broken.

◆

Kari Bodnarchuk, 32, travel writer/adventurer, Boston, Massachusetts

nets. For instance, are you an idealist? Prone to political activism? Keep in mind that many countries do not have the democratic liberties of the U.S., and that getting involved in the local politics of a foreign country can be quite dangerous. My advice: Don't. Better to save your hard-core activism for U.S. soil, where you know the rules, the consequences of breaking them, and where help is closer at hand if you need it.

➤ Make smart choices and use your common sense. Don't be paranoid, but be aware that bad things do happen and protect yourself.

➤ Most of the people who offer you food or drink are just being kind. However, the rare exception exists—drugging occasionally happens. Don't leave your drink unattended in bars, and exercise good judgment when accepting food or drink from people.

➤ Be aware of your vulnerabilities as a young woman on the road. For instance, in Indonesia, it is common for gigolos to prey on young female travelers. Don't be naïve about the intentions of foreign men.

> Alarming reports confirm an incease in date rape drugging. Increasingly young women in foreign countries and the US have a drink with a stranger and wake up the next morning, nude, raped, and robbed. They have no recollection of what happened. Rophynol, "the date rape drug," is odorless, tasteless, and colorless. It is a tranquilizer that can be easily slipped into your drink. Do not accept a drink that you didn't see poured. Do not leave your glass unattended.
>
> ◆
>
> *MBB*

➤ Are you in the mood for love? Make sure it's safe. AIDS is a growing crisis in many developing countries—ALWAYS use a condom.

➤ If you think you are pregnant, get a test. If it is positive, have a second test and then travel to a Western country (like Australia or England) or come home to deal with your options.

➤ How do you know when you've overstayed your welcome at someone's house? Trust your instincts. Servas International, a cultural exchange program, imposes a two-night minimum so you get to know your hosts, and your stay can last as long as it works for both parties. Leave before it is time.

➤ Stay flexible and remember that you can always come home. There's a lot of pressure to continue your travels, but if you're not enjoying yourself, if the trip is not what you expected, you can change your plans en route or come home. Sometimes just giving yourself permission to come home will clarify that you really want to continue traveling. Or you might realize you're just not ready for India yet, and that's okay too. Remember, being gutsy is about being true to yourself.

Don't panic when the unexpected occurs. Breathe, regain your bearings, and make an attempt to adapt. Easier said than done, but you would be surprised how an involuntary change of plans matched with some courage can actually enhance your trip. Embrace the unexpected! Isn't that why you ventured forth in the first place?

◆

Saki Bailey, 19, student, Santa Barbara, California

XIII
THE SOLO TRAVELER

Traveling alone is not lonely; it's an extremely powerful feeling, very similar to love—it's that kind of strength. It's partly the joy of total aloneness—not loneliness—of being part of the land, as far as you can see and knowing there's nobody you need share it with.

—*Christina Dodwell,* Travels with Pegasus

WHEN I STARTED TRAVELING ALONE, at age twenty-nine, it was not by choice. I couldn't find anyone to travel with me. I had two options: stay at home and give up my dream, or go alone. So I swallowed hard, bit my lower lip, and told the world and myself that I could do it. I would do it. I would go alone. I did. And I loved it! I traveled solo for the next two years around the world.

Starting out alone does not mean staying alone. There are many other fascinating people out there traveling by themselves, just like you. At times I would hook up with a kindred spirit and we would travel together for a few days, even for a month. Many of these travel companions are still close friends. My decision to go alone was one of the best choices of my life.

What's so great about it? Solo travelers enjoy the freedom of making all the decisions, experience the world unfiltered by anyone else's perspective, live intensely, meet people more easily and are invited into their lives more readily, avoid difficult travel companions, and get in touch with themselves.

> I have many opportunities to take my husband along on my travels and often do. But when I travel alone, it's an entirely different trip. Instead of being focused on the person with you, you are more observant, more attuned to every sound and detail. And you are much more likely to meet people.
>
> ◆
>
> *Kimberly Brown, 35, freelance writer/editor, Seattle, Washington*

Now when I create the opportunity to travel alone, it is a self-indulgent luxury. If you give it a fair chance, you too will discover that solo travel is empowering, intense, and exhilarating.

Divorce or the death of a spouse or partner can leave an avid traveler faced with the same dilemma I had. Do you choose to stay immobilized? Can you find a new travel companion? Or should you go alone? Eventually you'll begin doing day trips alone. In time you may move on to overnights, then longer journeys, until you are surprised and pleased by how confident and happy you are traveling alone.

TIPS

My marriage dissolved when I was forty-two. That marked the first time I put on a backpack. I knew I had to begin tackling the things I was most afraid of doing alone and travel was number one on my list. I spent five weeks on the road and remember crying a lot. But I also laughed a great deal! I'm fifty-six at this point. I've been traveling solo all this time, except now I wouldn't have it any other way.

◆

Evelyn Hannon, 56, editor,
Journeywoman, *Toronto, Canada*

➤ You can begin traveling solo at any age. Fortunate are the women who begin traveling alone when they were young. Often they tell me they never experienced any trepidation. For those of you who aren't too sure—try it. Don't let fear stop you. Other travelers on the road and local people will support you and you'll discover how much inner strength you possess.

➤ Consider taking a short trip first to see if you like traveling alone. Find a cute town close by and visit for the weekend. Bring something to read, a journal, and some CDs. Explore your surroundings. Be aware of your solitude and how it feels to be on your own. Then, if you're ready, plan a more adventurous trip. It's O.K. to start small.

➤ Start smart. Even if you want to be unstructured, book at least the first night's accommodation in advance. It will be easier to feel comfortable and get your bearings.

➤ When you travel alone, you accept the responsibility to reach out, be extroverted, and strike up conversations with strangers. You'll find it is much easier to make new friends when you are alone. You are more approachable.

➤ Trust your intuition, no matter what. You will have many great opportunities to explore new places and meet exciting people. One of the best things about travel is being open to these experiences. Just pay attention to your gut when you find yourself in a new situation. It will tell you when to go for it and when to get out. Always listen to your instincts and they will help keep you safe in the midst of your adventures.

➤ Women traveling alone share similar concerns about loneliness, safety, harassment, illness, and accidents. Don't worry. Going alone is not necessarily more dangerous than traveling with a companion—it just requires extra awareness. You will discover how fine-tuned

Everything was magnified by my being alone. In India, exploring a new city on foot, so pleasant in Europe, meant running the gauntlet: hawkers, beggars, insistent merchants came to me from everywhere, invading my personal space. With a companion, such scenes might have been merely local color. A twosome, self-contained, has its own resources. Through conversation and feed-back, it can defuse the impact of the unfamiliar in a way that the solo traveler cannot. Alone and uninitiated, I felt like Snow White assaulted by Disney's animated trees. Every experience was intensely my own, undiluted by the connection to home that a familiar companion supplies. Occasionally I thought, no one on earth knows where I am. That one point held both the exhilaration and the vulnerability of traveling alone.

◆

Jo Broyles Yohay, 56, writer, New York City, in Travelers' Tales: A Woman's World

your survival instincts are. Most countries in the world are not as violent or dangerous as our own. If you need help, ask for it.

➢ Don't travel alone into the backcountry—make sure at least one or two others accompany you. A backcountry injury without someone to help can pose a life-or-death situation.

➢ Buy a popular guidebook. The accommodations and restaurants listed will be full of other independent travelers, so you'll have plenty of opportunities to hook up with a variety of people. You may find yourself exploring the bazaar or eating a meal with your new friends, or you might even travel for a time together. Use your guidebook as an indication of things to see and where to start your journey, then travel farther off the beaten path.

➢ Don't isolate yourself in a hotel or rental car. It's much easier to meet people if you are out and about with locals and other travelers. Use public transportation and stay in hostels, local homes, or bed-and-breakfasts. You will probably meet so many people that you just might yearn for some time alone!

➢ Check out the meeting places for independent travelers. Some guidebooks (such as the Lonely Planet series) will list them. Many cities have well-known meccas for independent travelers, with bulletin boards and unique calendars of local events. These are treasure troves of inex-

One of my most memorable encounters in Sri Lanka would not have occurred if I had not been alone and not accepted the kind offer of help from strangers. I was waiting at what I believed to be a bus stop when a man in a battered station wagon filled with cheerful kids stopped and offered me a ride. He informed me that where I was standing was not a bus stop. I accepted his offer because of the presence of his four children. His invitation for a ride to my guesthouse led to a dinner with his wife and a schoolteacher, tours of the island, and a charming friendship.

◆

MBB

pensive tours, travel companions or rides wanted, free or almost-free local lectures, and social gatherings, that you can join. A morning jog with the running group "Hash House Harriers" in

Singapore or Kathmandu can lead to local friends and social invitations. My hand-written note posted on a message board on a tree in the café courtyard of the Old Stanley Hotel in Nairobi led to a safari with wonderful people and dynamic friendships.

> Every time we set foot on our own as solo travelers, we shave off the edge of oddness and anomaly. We are seen enjoying ourselves, taking care of ourselves. We pave the way for normalcy someday for all those women peeking out from kitchen curtains and behind veils.
>
> ◆
>
> *Joan Medhurst, 49, retired professor, Alameda, California*

➤ Take advantage of your solo status and be willing to change your plans. One of the greatest things about traveling alone is that you get to do whatever you want to do, all the time. Make an impromptu side trip to the beach. Add an entire country to your anticipated itinerary. Stay in bed all morning on a rainy day. Revel in the joy of not having to compromise.

➤ Treat yourself to small luxuries like high tea at an elegant hotel or a manicure.

➤ When graciously offered, accept spontaneous invitations and hospitality, especially from women or families. Be careful, however, not to overstay your welcome or create a hardship for the family.

➤ How do you handle eating alone in a restaurant? Choose a bistro, café, or lively place. Go prepared with reading and writing materials—postcards, letters, and your journal. Comfortably dining alone is a learned skill. Eventually you'll find yourself enjoying watching people and eavesdropping. And you won't always stay alone after being seated in a restaurant. I have often been invited to join other travelers or vice versa.

➤ Don't be afraid to eavesdrop. It's a great way to identify interesting people with whom you might share something in common. Find a sneaky way to join the conversation.

TIPS FOR OVERCOMING THAT LONELY FEELING

➢ I am often asked, "Do you ever get lonely, and what do you do about it?" I am surprised by how rarely I do get lonely. Remember, just because you are traveling alone doesn't mean you'll be more lonesome than at home.

➢ Fear of being lonely is common and can stop you cold in your tracks. To assuage fears, keep in mind that loneliness is a bit like PMS—predictable, irritating, and temporary.

➢ Different moments in your trip will require different approaches to coping with loneliness. Sometimes it's important not to sink into your loneliness. To counter loneliness, stay active. Take a walk in a park, eat in lively, crowded restaurants, initiate conversations with strangers, and shop for gifts for your friends and family. Other times giving in to your mood is the best possible medicine. At times like this, I become reclusive, reading, listening to music, writing in my journal or to friends and family.

> ———— ⚓ ————
>
> I missed meeting a friend at the Lisbon train station and discovered the world of solo travel. Now, I wouldn't have it any other way. Traveling alone, I think the smells are sharper, the sounds more distinct, the flavors more powerful, and the people much friendlier.
>
> ◆
>
> *Kari Bodnarchuk, 32, travel writer/adventurer, Boston, Massachusetts*

➢ When you're feeling low, I don't recommend calling home. It can make you feel worse. But writing postcards or sending an e-mail from a cybercafé is uplifting.

➢ Take care of yourself. When I start to feel lonely, it's often because I haven't eaten or slept enough or I've had too much caffeine. If I stay well fed, fit, and rested, then depression, loneliness, and illness are usually avoided.

➤ Treat yourself. I will pamper myself with a hot bubble bath, buy a new book and dig into it, or have a massage or manicure. In India and Thailand I bought garlands of gardenias and richly fragrant flowers for my room. In Chicago I got dressed up and went to a posh hotel for a drink and hours of people watching.

➤ Write in a journal. When you find yourself missing your best friend at home, write down everything you want to tell her in your journal. Don't just put down what you saw that day—include how you're feeling about yourself and your trip. If you want to go home, write about it! Periodically read back over your journal and see how your journey is unfolding. Take yourself out to dinner when you realize how fabulous you are!

> _____ ⚘ _____
>
> Recognize the difference between solitude and loneliness. I made the choice to be alone and I like my own company. Now I cherish my time alone and accept the lonely moments. They never last long. They come and go, just like at home.
>
> ◆
>
> *MBB*

➤ Give your friends and family addresses where they can send you letters and packages. Even in this age of e-mail, there's nothing like a handwritten letter or mom's cookies to make you feel at home! Mail can be sent "poste restante" to a town's main post office or to an American Express office (all you need are a few travelers' checks to use their service). Most places will hold your mail for a month or so and can also forward it on to your next destination for a nominal fee.

XIV
WOMEN TRAVELING TOGETHER

One of the great things about travel is you find out how many good,
kind people there are.

—*Edith Wharton*

AT MY SPEAKING ENGAGEMENTS the conversation inevitably turns toward women traveling together. For many women, traveling with other women takes the fear out of seeing the world. Women always ask how they can meet other women travel companions. They are single, divorced, or widowed; their husbands aren't interested in travel; or their friends won't travel without their husbands. Now more than ever women are interested in finding other women to travel with.

I encourage women to meet other women for the sole purpose of travel. Find someone who shares your passion for wandering the globe or for weekend getaways. Or meet someone local who has similar interests—for example, photography—and go on a photography travel expedition together. There are many travel companies that specialize in planning trips specifically for women (see the Resources section for more information). These trips are a lot of fun and chances are you will meet others that you might want to travel with in the future.

A different kind of bonding unfolds on an all-women trip. Last spring I traveled for twelve days in France with seven women I didn't know. I laughed more in those twelve days than I had in the last twelve months. Traveling with women is a different and wonderful kind of fun. So if you're married and your husband doesn't like to travel, leave him at home. He'll be there when you get back.

♦

MBB

New friendships are formed on the road, and life-long relationships deepened. A getaway with your girlfriends can be a wonderful thing, one that will remind you why you've been friends for so long. It gives you a chance to spend quality time together and gives you an increased comfort level while traveling. When you travel with other women, be open to self-discovery and self-revelation. Get to know the women you are traveling with and share your life experiences with them. This part of the journey holds wonderful possibilities. Enjoy your time bonding with the other women on the trip, and be open to meeting even more women in the destinations to which you are traveling.

TIPS

➤ Before you and your travel companions leave, acknowledge that problems may arise and discuss how you will deal with them. Be honest about your "hot buttons" (people being bossy, chronic lateness) and agree to be sensitive to each other's particular needs. Be open when something is bothering you and address it immediately. Talk issues through and don't let them fester. Then let them go and enjoy your trip.

➤ When traveling with others, it's always good to set boundaries before you go. If you know that you need personal quiet time each day, then be sure to articulate this to your travel partner. That way she won't take it personally and will know that you simply need your space. See "Roommate Rules" below for more information.

➤ Don't assume that you can borrow your travel partner's make-up, brush, shampoo, conditioner, toothpaste, or clothes. Just because you are traveling together, that doesn't mean her items are up for grab. Be respectful and ask permission if you would like to borrow something.

➤ To make more room in your luggage, discuss items that you might be able to share with your traveling companion. She can bring the hair dryer, and you'll pack the binoculars.

➤ Take off on your own for a few days. You might be interested in exploring Venice, while she would rather stay in Florence. Don't limit your itinerary. Travel solo and arrange to reconvene at a specific time and place.

➤ Seek out women to talk to while you travel—on trains, in restaurants or cafés, or while shopping. You will learn a lot from local women that will enhance your travels. They are usually as pleased to meet you as you are to meet them.

➤ If you want to meet women in larger cities, make a quick check of local directories under the headings "female," "woman," or "travel." This can produce wonders. You'll probably find listings for craft collectives, women's bookstores, and women's organizations.

➤ If you are a lesbian traveling with your significant other and you are worried about the treatment you will receive if the nature of your relationship is known, then do not reveal the truth. In some cultures, it may be better to hide your relationship than take the risk of being harassed, mistreated, or physically harmed.

ROOMMATE RULES

➤ When you find out who your roommate will be, call her and introduce yourself. This is a good time to tell her a bit about yourself and delicately and honestly to approach the topic of snoring. Ask her, "Do you snore?" Better to find out before the trip and take along earplugs, or find another roommate, than to find out the first sleepless night.

➤ On the first day establish ground rules, including showering times, choosing beds, storage space, and dividing the bathroom counter space. That way there is no misunderstanding.

➤ Describe your preferred "morning mood." I am silent and greatly appreciate quiet or soft conversations; I like to exercise in the morning, so when you wake up I may be gone. This way she won't worry if she wakes up and you aren't there.

➤ Promise to give one another some time alone in the room every day. This should be a minimum of thirty minutes. Set up an agreeable schedule ahead of time, and when it is your turn to give your roommate her time, go for a walk, read, or write post-cards in the lobby or a local café.

➤ Just because you are roommates, you don't have to spend all of your time together. Communicate clearly that you came on the trip to meet a lot of new people.

When I travel with a companion, I always pack at least one outfit in their suitcase, and vice-versa. That way, if one set of luggage gets lost or delayed, we're not without a change of clothes.

◆

Joyce Sosebee, 61, Woodside, California

XV
THE OLDER ADVENTURER

Age is not determined by the passing of years, but by our reactions to new ideas—our resistance to change. People grow old through their encasement in the past—not in their hopes for the future. Years may wrinkle the skin; but to give up faith, courage, ambition, enthusiasm for the future, and the spark of continuing growth wrinkles the soul!

—*Pacific Crest Outward Bound School,* Book of Readings

IN MY GRANDMOTHER'S DAY, the only acceptable travel for a middle-aged or older woman was to visit Aunt Pearl or her grown children. Normal women in their fifties, sixties, and seventies didn't hike in New Zealand, bike in New England, join a study tour to Spain, or travel alone! Bus tours and cruise ships were the predominant form of senior travel. Society has changed. Today, as seniors stay more active and mature women become more gutsy, your imagination is the limit.

An experienced septuagenarian traveler, Betty Ann Webster, once told me, "I have traveled with my husband and children, with friends of many countries, with a forty-year-old son, and enjoyed all those trips. I've often found white hair and advanced age an advantage. For instance, I am never hassled by men as younger women traveling by themselves sometimes are. On the contrary, I'm often helped, whether I need it or not. Young Asians call me 'Aunty.' I have never encountered violence, either physical or verbal. Traveling, especially alone, involves risk, trust, judgment, and probably luck. But doesn't life itself, wherever you are?"

> Age is no barrier to your dreams and goals.
>
> ◆
>
> *Helen Thayer, 50, skied solo to the North Pole, author of* Polar Dream

Grandparents are also spending valuable time with their grandchildren traveling. Travel presents an invaluable opportunity to get to know your grandchildren in unique contexts. Indeed, more and more intergenerational families are taking to the road, the skies, the seas, and the rails...and loving it. Everyone is enriched by cross-generational bonding, grandparent mentoring, and different generations learning and exploring together.

No matter how old you are, it's never too late to travel.

TIPS

➤ The world's your oyster! If you're retired, you can travel any season and, if you want, avoid other tourists. Take advantage of your flexibility.

➤ If you plan to travel with a group, at the time you're doing your research be sure to ask about "single supplements." Several soft adventure travel companies will not charge you an extra fee if they cannot find you a roommate. (See Resources section for names, addresses, and phone numbers of tour operators.)

➤ Look for special-interest tours and groups or organize a journey around a special passion.

➤ Ask the tour company for a list of passengers who have gone on the tour you wish to take. Call several of them and ask them what they thought of the trip.

> At age sixty, I flew with a friend to Jasper, Alberta, and we rode our bikes to Denver—1,800 miles. We crossed the Continental Divide six times. Before we left, everyone told us not to go, that it wouldn't be safe for two women alone. In five weeks no harm came to us. One of the important things I learned was how material things can become an encumbrance and how little you need to get along. I recommend to anyone, any age, if you have a dream, you mustn't put it off five years. Everybody, please, follow your dreams.
>
> ◆
>
> *Mary Mulligan, 63, bookseller, Tattered Cover Bookstore, Denver, Colorado*

➤ Youth hostels are not just for youth. They offer safe, clean, friendly lodging all over the world.

➤ Traveling by recreational vehicle is increasingly popular with many elder adventurers. Consider renting an RV to try it out. You can become a member of an RV association and travel with other RVers or learn RV maintenance.

➤ A medical emergency abroad can be quite frightening. Take out trip insurance that offers emergency evacuation.

➤ Carry a list of phone numbers and addresses for U.S. embassies and consulates in the region in which you're traveling. You can contact them for emergency services. They can also help you find a reputable local doctor, dentist, or hospital.

➤ As an older traveler, the deals await you! Travel presents a great opportunity to flaunt your age and save your money. Just remember to ask if there's a senior deal.

> ___ ⋆ ___
>
> On recent trips to Turkey and British Columbia, I wore a fanny pack instead of carrying a purse. The relief I felt in never worrying "Where is my purse?" was inestimable
>
> ◆
>
> *Ruth Bond, 78, retired schoolteacher, Hudson, Ohio*

> ___ ⋆ ___
>
> As a senior citizen, you should know that Medicare does not cover medical expenses overseas. When you travel, be sure to get a policy that will cover you while you are abroad.
>
> ◆
>
> *Olga Murray, 75, president, Nepal Youth Opportunity Foundation, Sausalito, California*

ON THE ROAD WITH THE GRANDKIDS

➤ Share stories of the "olden days." Relate historic events—the Model T, the first moon landing, Woodstock, and so forth—to your grandchildren's studies.

➤ Tell your grandchildren stories about their mom and dad when they were young—this can create a strong link between past and present. Try the following theme: "Let me tell you a story about when your (mother or father) was bad." Children take special delight in hearing about the behavior of their parents, especially the naughty stuff.

➢ Take a lot of pictures and videos.

➢ Set rules you are comfortable with, even if they are different from their parents'.

➢ You might need more downtime than those feisty squirts—take the grandkids to a park so they can meet children their own age.

A delightful side effect of developing a shock of white hair is that other travelers often feel a need to help an older woman. Never mind that I'm on my way to shoot the rapids of a wild New Zealand river or explore an ancient shipwreck with a scuba partner. When I patiently listen to a teenager giving directions to a place from which I've just come, it creates a bond that invites further interaction. I've made friendships, uncovered new places, sampled exotic fare, just because for a moment I traded my need to assert self-assurance for the exhilaration of discovery.

◆

Judy Wade, 50, travel writer/ photographer, Phoenix, Arizona

There is no age barrier to finding a new direction in life. At 65 I took my "point and shoot" camera to the Galapagos and was surprised with the results. So on my next trip—to Tibet—I took a more sophisticated camera that I knew very little about. I discovered a new career in nature photography. Age means nothing when you are doing something you love. Keeping fit is key and when you find something that moves you, like travel does, go for it.

◆

Marge Samilson, 73, wildlife photographer, Tiburon, California

XVI
MOTHER-DAUGHTER TRAVEL

From grandma and her maternal line, I inherited the urge to keep moving.
For the women in my family, getting away from the ordinary provides
impetus to wander. Travel exemplifies freedom.

Vera Marie Badertscher, "Traveling Woman," A Mother's World

MORE AND MORE WOMEN are taking to the road in mother-daughter pairs. And with good reason. If you want to know about the inner life of your mother or daughters, you need almost endless opportunities to talk. The journey you take will be to the center of yourself and your relationship. The memories you will cherish for a lifetime.

I was twenty-six when my mother and I took our first trip together—just the two of us. She left my dad in Ohio and came to visit me. We spent the weekend exploring gold-mining towns in the foothills of the Sierra Nevada mountains. We talked and laughed almost every waking moment. Quite by accident, we came upon a river-rafting group preparing to ride the rapids down the Stanislaus River. Without a moment's hesitation, my mother said, "I've always wanted to do this. Let's see if we

> Laura and I have a wonderful time traveling together, but at times it is a challenge for me to travel "college style." Laura, of course, does not have any trouble adjusting to the luxury hotels to which I've become accustomed. The pleasure of traveling with my daughter is how her openness to new adventures off the beaten path affects me.
>
> ♦
>
> *Lenore Thornton, 51,*
> *investment advisor, New York City*

can join them!" We spent the afternoon shooting the rapids. And I spent months reflecting upon how little I knew about my responsible, schoolteacher mother.

Few things are more rewarding, so don't hesitate to do it.

TIPS

➤ Offer your mother the priceless gift of your time. Treat her to a night away—just the two of you. Plan an activity that will be very special for both of you: an elegant dinner, a play, a nice hotel, or a river-rafting trip.

➤ If your short excursions together are successful, consider traveling together for longer periods, perhaps even booking an organized tour to someplace you both have always wanted to go.

➤ Begin an annual tradition of taking your mother or daughter, or both, on an overnight adventure. Try camping if you enjoy the outdoors or stay at a resort close to home. You might choose a date near Mother's Day or her birthday.

> _Traveling with my mother in Hawaii made me realize that our physical capabilities weren't at the same level anymore. We both had to learn to respect her limitations and find alternatives that we could both enjoy._
>
> ◆
>
> _Nancy Lowenherz, 33, director of public relations, Chicago, Illinois_

➤ Be honest up front about how to avoid stepping on one another's toes. If your mom hates the way you drive, hand over the keys. If you're miserable unless you have a window seat, let her know before she books the tickets. Talking openly about your trip in advance will allow you to focus on enjoying your time together.

➤ Give one another space. Just because you're on a trip together doesn't mean that you

> _I travel with my mother. I learned it's best not to share a hotel room because she's a light sleeper and likes to read and have a cup of tea at 4 A.M. She also rearranges my clothes in the closet. I let her read all the historic road signs and she lets me drive over the speed limit._
>
> ◆
>
> _Virginia Sheridan, 40+, president, M. Silver Associates, New York City_

have to spend every moment in shared company. Create time in the day for each of you to do your own thing. At times you may consider getting separate rooms so you can have the evening to quietly reflect and reenergize.

➤ Bring along books and music that you can enjoy together. If you're on a longer trip, you and your mother can each bring a few books and then trade. Discuss your opinions of your shared readings during long rides and over meals.

➤ If your mother is a widow and you are single, and you usually spend the holidays together, consider exploring a new corner of the world instead of staying home. A friend of mine, a widow in her seventies, and her daughter, in her thirties, spend every Christmas holiday making memories—from tramping around Anasazi ruins in the Southwest to cruising in the Indonesian islands.

➤ If you can work it out, take your daughter on a short business trip. You can show her what your professional life is like away from home and how you use caution to navigate safely in an unfamiliar city. You can share the places you enjoy, such as museums, parks, cafés, and restaurants.

> ───── ⚶ ─────
>
> For me, the best thing about traveling with my momma is sharing a bed and cuddling.
>
> ◆
>
> *Annalyse Sheppard, 5,*
> *Marin, California*

➤ One of the most rewarding aspects of taking a mother-daughter trip is the way we travel. We dawdle along the road; we pause to stop and stare; we relax over a pot of tea, watching people, being quiet or talking about the idiosyncrasies of life. Be sure to allow for unstructured time in your itinerary.

➤ If you are traveling with your mother, ask her about her youth, her teenage years, her romances. Share some of your more private memories with her.

➤ Take your mom on the trip she fantasizes about. If she's always wanted to see her grandmother's birthplace in Mexico, surprise her with a plane ticket and your companionship.

➤ I try to take each of my daughters individually on a mother-daughter outing every year. I love these trips. They give me the opportunity to focus on one child at a time and appreciate how she is growing and our relationship is changing. There is no sibling rivalry and she has all of my attention. The sibling left at home, of course, is being spoiled rotten by her dad, who is having special father-daughter time with her. It is healthy for everyone in the family. Don't wait until they're grown.

_____ ☀ _____

The best thing about my travels with my mother is that I am always expecting to show her my world and my experiences, living in another country (Thailand), but instead we end up creating new experiences and discovering a world of our own.

◆

Laura Thornton, 30,
foreign democracy monitor,
Bangkok, Thailand

_____ ☀ _____

Mama's passport photo says it all. The impish grin is brighter than the white curls, the wrinkle of smile deeper than the wrinkles of age. She's happy. She's going somewhere. With me. The mug shot proves I shouldn't have waited so long to invite her. We'd talked about a big trip we'd take "sometime," but I married and got even busier at home and work, and summers and years passed with no adventure together. Then Daddy died. Out of those sad days of winter came a sense of urgency. Time and life were galloping past, and I needed to catch up.

◆

Mary Ellen Botter, 52, assistant travel editor, Dallas Morning News, *Prosper, Texas*

XVII
TRAVEL WITH CHILDREN

It is a wise parent who gives her children roots and wings.
—*Chinese Proverb*

———

BEFORE WE HAD KIDS, my husband and I were sure our style of travel wouldn't change; we would just haul our children with us—everywhere. But along with the sleepless nights, diapers, bibs, blankets, and colic came a foreboding premonition that I would never travel again in any way. Although my children haven't exactly stopped me, they have slowed me down (sometimes for the better). I have learned when to take them along and when to go alone.

I am a strong advocate of numerous family vacations each year. Unfortunately, our trips are usually short. But I feel almost any getaway is worth the hassle.

Let me clarify what I mean by *family*. I don't just mean the "Ozzie and Harriet" nuclear family of mom, dad, and 2.4 children. Today's family may be any combination of children with a single parent, significant others, friends, or grandparents.

> ——— ⋰⋰⋰ ———
>
> Traveling with kids under six is fun. All you have to do is keep them fed and rested.
>
> ◆
>
> *Rebecca Frank, 47, Colorado*
> *wildlife commissioner,*
> *Grand Junction, Colorado*

Some of the gutsiest women I know and admire are single moms who travel with their children all the time, almost everywhere. At a book signing in Fairlawn, Ohio, a single mom told me her story of driving to Alaska with her three-year-old daughter and camping for two months. I was humbled by her courage. She was still amazed and empowered by her adventure. Such stories are not unusual. I applaud every mom who has taken her children camping or traveling on her own.

Traveling with children is very different from traveling by yourself, with your spouse, or with a friend. Although you may, as I did, have great trepidation about traveling with your children, you will soon learn that the rewards and memories are worth every inconvenience. My children have opened up new worlds for me. They have given me a different and refreshing perspective on everything we do and see. Together we make more friends and feed off each other's energy and adventurous spirits.

> Traveling is your children's best teacher. When they observe how other people live in other places, they not only learn about the wider world but about their world, too. Just don't expect them to express their thanks for the trips you've taken together. Appreciation will only come later in life.
>
> ♦
>
> *Claire Walter, editor/travel writer, Boulder, Colorado*

TIPS

➤ Everyone should be involved—from planning the trip and packing to making decisions on the road. As soon as you know where you are going, involve your children: check out books and magazines from your library, mark up a map, discuss what distance you will travel, how long it will take to get there, and what they will do during this time. Let the kids take part in the selection of the toys, games, books, and art materials you take along.

➤ Children learn responsibility when they compose their own packing lists and pack their own bags. It builds confidence and decision-making skills. Show them your lists and discuss how you are packing and making plans in advance. They can make sure that their favorite clothes are clean the day before departure. It is a good idea to confirm that they have the essentials.

➤ Plan age-appropriate activities. Each day should include something of interest for everyone. Take into consideration your youngest child's interests and abilities and then work your way through the interests of each family member, including yourself.

➤ Rest and relaxation should be high on your list of activities. Plan quiet time or naps. Picnics are a great way to slow down your pace. Find a park where they can run around and meet other kids while you put your feet up and read some of your book.

➤ Keep it simple. Underplan your days and move at a leisurely pace so you don't feel rushed. Traveling with children, you won't be able to see or do as much as you would without them. They need extra time to get dressed, go to the bathroom, have snacks, and work off extra energy.

> ___ ⋙ ___
>
> Traveling with children requires not only love but extra patience and ingenuity, especially ingenuity, to keep them occupied and to replace the comforting routines of home.
>
> ◆
>
> *Ruth Bond, 78, retired schoolteacher, Hudson, Ohio*

➤ You can simplify your life if you locate and use the restrooms as soon as you arrive at an attraction or museum.

➤ Snacks and filling food are essential. If you feed them, they will be happy. At all times carry drinks and stick-to-your-ribs snacks like apples, bagels, or low-fat granola bars.

➤ It is helpful to set expectations for a vacation prior to departure. Discuss how things will be different where you are going. Prepare your kids for new kinds of food, entertainment, toilets, languages, long

> ___ ⋙ ___
>
> On long car trips we always bring children's music and books on tape, as well as being prepared with other activities. We plan a special stop for a picnic along the way, which gives my sons something to look forward to. Always be flexible, and know you will inevitably make extra stops along the way.
>
> ◆
>
> *Amy Volin, 33, mother, Denver, Colorado*

travel days, and periods of "down time." Children are more agreeable if they know what to expect.

➢ On long trips, children get by with very few clothes or toys and they learn how little they really need to be happy. Encourage them to pack lightly.

➢ When traveling, children quickly learn that their favorite foods and entertainment are not available everywhere, and that some of their favorite foods may indeed be considered disgusting by others—and vice versa. Most kids will try new foods and abandon picky eating habits. They will discover new and simple ways to entertain themselves.

➢ If you are traveling long distances by car with small children, and you want to arrive at your destination with time to spare, rise at 4:30 or 5:00 A.M. and pack your vehicle before everyone else awakes. Pack swimsuits and pajamas in separate bags so they are easily accessible. This way you will not have to break down all your bags to get at one item.

➢ Learn some elements of the language as a family before you travel to a foreign country. Your children will not only benefit from beginning to learn a new language, they will get to use it practically and make friends more easily, even if they know only a few key phrases and words.

➢ If an extended trip is not possible, take your child to a local ethnic market or check out a culture-appropriate video from the library.

➢ History "sticks" when children actually see where it took place. Being in a noteworthy place makes a far stronger impression than most books can. Background material will enhance the experience, however, so check out relevant books from the library before you go.

➢ Stop at tourist information booths or offices. Your children can pick up brochures and create scrapbooks from them. You may also learn about a festival or museum—or cave—you were unaware of (and may discover a family member has an interest you never suspected).

➢ Travel teaches kids to take pleasure from exploring the natural world—watching a tide pool, collecting pinecones to make forest dolls, rolling down grassy hillsides, seeing an eagle hunt. Try to spend unstructured time outdoors.

➢ Trips are a great way to make geography come alive. Show your children the intended route on the map and explain how long it will take to go from point A to point B. Use city and state maps for shorter excursions. Get a felt-tip pen and draw your route; it will be a wonderful souvenir and memory prompt later, even if it is in tatters.

➢ Kids learn about other cultures by exposure to them: attending a rodeo in Wyoming, observing a tribal powwow in New Mexico, staying in a home in Ireland, visiting a pottery workshop in Mexico, meandering through a market in any developing country, or buying hot, fresh tortillas at a *tortilleria* in Baja.

> In our family, we have a slogan: "If it is free, we go and see; if you have to pay, we stay away." State parks, national forest campgrounds, and motels in small towns are bargains.
>
> ◆
>
> *Doris Scharfenberg, 71, freelance writer, Farmington Hills, Michigan*

➢ For really picky eaters, consider offering the child a coin in the local currency for every new food they try. Is this a bribe? Yes!

➢ Kids need lots of physical activity. Carry action toys—such as a frisbee, inflatable beach ball, or tennis ball—with you at all times for an impromptu sports game.

➢ Buy postcards in the airport or in gift shops and bring stationery. Travel time is great for writing to pen pals, friends, or grandparents.

➤ Travel teaches children how to be flexible as the family encounters delays, cancellations, reservation mix-ups, closed attractions, full restaurants, rude people. They will learn to remain calm and enjoy the adventure if *you* do.

➤ Memories are made from such brief moments. A trip of only a few short days or weeks in reality will last a lifetime. Children will never forget learning how to make a campfire, bathing under a waterfall, eating mangoes on the beach under a full moon, walking across an airport tarmac, or mimicking unforgettable characters on the road.

> ———— ⚜ ————
>
> When you arrive at a museum, head for the gift ship. Have your children look through the postcards depicting artwork in the museum's collection and pick out five of their favorites, then have them search for them on your tour of the museum. This makes the visit much more enjoyable.
>
> ◆
>
> *Carole Terwilliger Meyers, 50, author, Oakland, California*

➤ Traveling together will change your family. You will discover each other as individuals and appreciate each other's unique characteristics. So keep a record of the trip and the changes you observe in each other. Describe funny situations, conversations, and memorable comments that each person makes in your travel journal.

> ———— ⚜ ————
>
> Traveling with my daughters to an art museum is different than when I was a child. I allow my girls to speak out and explore. If you stop and see things through their eyes, as opposed to making them see the world through adult eyes, you will learn something not only about the world, but about each other. This is a travel experience you will bring home and keep for life.
>
> ◆
>
> *Christine Loomis, 44, writer/editor, Boulder, Colorado*

SAFETY FIRST

➤ In a car, always buckle up your children, no matter how much they protest. A person is four times more likely to be killed and thirteen times more likely to be injured when thrown from a car.

➤ Keep your baby in the car safety seat. Stop if you have to feed or comfort your baby. A 10-pound infant in a three mile per hour crash would be ripped from your arms with a force of 200 pounds.

➤ Safety belts are made for one person. Children should not share them.

➤ Don't use pillows or cushions to boost your child.

➤ Stop for frequent rests, exercising, and toilet breaks.

➤ Children should carry their own identification inside their packs, in purses, or sewn into their clothing.

➤ Kids and ticks go together like peanut butter and jelly. Although most ticks are harmless, Lyme disease, caused by the bite of a rare and tiny tick, is a serious concern for every parent. Be prepared when hiking in unfamiliar areas. Prevention is not always easy. It is recommended that you and your kids wear long sleeves and long pants in the woods and grassy areas. Take a shower after being outside and check yourself and your child carefully.

➤ If you do find a tick, remove it gently but firmly with tweezers. Take your time. If you pull too hard or twist, you may leave the head embedded in the body. Wipe the skin with antiseptic. Keep the tick. Put it in a jar to show medical authorities later if necessary. Watch for any skin reaction or any unusual symptoms and contact a physician immediately if they occur.

➤ On family vacations it seems that everyone gets a large dose of sunshine, but sunburn for a child is serious. Pack lots of sunscreen (SPF fifteen or greater); use it thirty minutes before going into the sun and reapply every two hours, even if the product is touted as waterproof. Cloudy days are just as dangerous as sunny days.

➤ Always pack a broad-brimmed hat or bonnet to protect your child's face, ears, and scalp. Keep babies out of the sun entirely.

➤ Bees love sweets, watermelon, and burgers. So do kids. What do you do when the two meet? Remove the stinger with a horizontal scraping motion, using your fingernail or something flat like a driver's license. Don't squeeze or pull the stinger or you'll release more venom. Clean the site with soap and water and apply ice compresses. Make a paste of unseasoned meat tenderizer or baking soda (if you happen to have some with you) and water and apply to the area. This will neutralize the remaining venom.

➤ When traveling with kids your first-aid kit should include tweezers (with pointed tips), bandages, gauze, fancy Band-aids, antibacterial soap, adhesive tape, first aid/antibacterial cream or ointment, child- and adult-strength ibuprofen or aspirin, syrup of ipecac (for poison), thermometer, age-appropriate motion sickness medication, sunscreen, and antihistamine for allergic reactions. A bottle of unseasoned meat tenderizer is handy for bee or wasp stings. Zip-lock bags make quick ice packs with a hand towel for a cover.

➤ When you arrive at theme parks, museums, and other crowded tourist attractions, select a central meeting place just in case you get separated from your kids. Counsel them on how to identify and approach an employee to ask for help if they think they are lost. If they need to locate you in a crowd, advise them to call you by your first names. There will be lots of other mommies and daddies.

➤ Have your children memorize the name of your hotel. Give them a hotel business card to keep in their pocket.

➤ Encourage your kids to wear bright-colored tops so they are more visible in a crowd.

XVIII

SPECIAL-INTEREST AND VOLUNTEER PROGRAMS

Never doubt that a small group of thoughtful, committed citizens can change the world. Indeed, it is the only thing that ever has.

—*Margaret Mead*

SOMETIMES UNSTRUCTURED, FREE-WHEELING TRAVEL is as good as it gets—a delicious break from the regimens of our busy, over-planned lives. Other times nothing surpasses the rewards of planting yourself in one place and digging in. For travel with a meaningful twist, consider volunteering or joining theme-oriented journeys.

If you're craving a deeper connection to the places you're visiting, ready to throw yourself into a project, and excited to meet and work with people from all over the world, I highly recommend volunteering during your travels. Volunteering on the road can require as minimal a commitment as a day or as extensive a commitment as a couple of years. It all depends on what you want to do and the flexibility of your plans. Yet, regardless of the length or nature of your volunteer stint, it will likely be one of the most rewarding parts of your trip. Volunteering feeds the soul. It immerses you more deeply than you could imagine and will leave its imprint long after the project ends.

Many international organiza-

Teaching in Japan gave me a depth of knowledge and insight into the culture that I would not otherwise have gained, even through years of study. While not always easy, nothing else I've done has been nearly as worthwhile or rewarding. I learned at least as much as I taught, and I left with some of the most vivid memories and deepest friendships of my life.

♦

Tara Weaver, 29, teacher/writer, San Francisco, California

tions offer an array of volunteer and work-abroad options as far-ranging as an archaeological dig in Israel, trail maintenance in Yellowstone National Park, school-building in Nicaragua, caring for the dying at Mother Teresa's hospice in Calcutta, museum restoration in England, and teaching English in Tunisia. Volunteer possibilities are innumerable—what matters is finding the right match for you.

TIPS

➤ Determine your interests, needs, and reasons for volunteering. The clearer you are about what you want, the more likely you'll choose your project well, and the less likely you'll feel disappointed or frustrated by your experience.

➤ Take into account your abilities and limitations—emotional, physical, intellectual, and financial. For instance, do you have a bad back? If so, a project involving hard manual labor and lots of bending—such as building a house—might not be for you. Likewise, if you're highly skilled at working with people, consider putting that ability to use in your volunteer work.

➤ Research the organizations you come across and try to avoid committing to the first opportunity that pops up. You want to know as much as possible about the organization with which you work and feel confident about what you're getting yourself into.

> Volunteering overseas gave me a new perspective on my own cultural values and assumptions. It made me more thoughtful about which ones I truly want to adopt.
>
> ◆
>
> *Tracy Hessel, Amigos de las Americas, in* How to Live Your Dream of Volunteering Overseas

➤ Talk to alumni of whatever organization/project you're considering. Some of the most honest and accurate evaluations of a program come from those who have gone before you, who have already invested their time, energy, and money. Their experience and wisdom is often invaluable.

➤ Find out how long the organization has been around. Is its work well respected? Will you feel good about having an affiliation with this organization?

➤ How much money are you willing or able to spend? The financial costs of volunteer projects vary considerably. Some volunteer opportunities are free, whereas others cost more than a package tour. Don't forget to take into account the cost of getting to the work location.

➤ How do you feel about groups? Most volunteer projects involve working closely with a group of strangers. (Of course they won't be strangers for long!) Working together can be one of the most rewarding ways to get to know people, including those from different countries and backgrounds, but also one of the most challenging. As with all travel, it helps to be flexible, open, and up for the adventure.

➤ Find out how much time you'll have to yourself. Will you have days off? An hour of solitary time each day? Or will most of your time be determined by the structure of the program? How many hours per day are you expected to work? Is there any flexibility?

➤ Are you traveling with your family? Ask if kids can participate. If not, is there something else for them to do in the area?

➤ Don't expect things to operate exactly as they do back home. While the differences

> —— ⋎⋏⋎ ——
>
> When you go to another country, not only do you take a fresh look at that country, you take a fresh look at your own country, and your own experience, and you never quite accept things the same way.
>
> ◆
>
> *Paula Morris, Voluntary Service Overseas, Zimbabwe and Indonesia, in* How to Live Your Dream of Volunteering Overseas

may be charming to the short-term visitor or tourist, those volunteering or working abroad for long stints may get frustrated when systems do not function in familiar ways. Be prepared and, when it happens, relax. This is an opportunity to learn how things work locally and how to approach the situation next time around.

➤ Realize that it may not be possible to accomplish as much as you initially planned—not that you shouldn't try! Language, cultural differences, tradition,

> ___ ⚶ ___
>
> I volunteered to work on a small organic farm in remote Far North Queensland, Australia. The work was hard, it poured every day, and I got attacked by biting ants. Still, I loved being outdoors all the time, doing valuable work, and getting way off the tourist track.
>
> ◆
>
> *Michelle Snider, 29, writer, Oakland, California*

and pace of life may prove challenging obstacles to your original objectives. If this happens, don't despair. Reevaluate your goals and focus on what is achievable, given the specifics of the situation. There is no failure in altering your plans once you've learned what is truly possible and worth pursuing.

➤ While travelers often exist in a constant state of discovery, when you settle into a place for longer stretches it is possible to slip into a daily pattern. Don't lose sight of the incredible opportunity you have to explore your host culture. Make a list of things you want to accomplish in your time overseas, whether it's studying traditional arts or languages, visiting specific places, or experiencing special events or festivals. By organizing your time and setting goals, you can make sure your time is well spent—it will be over before you know it!

➤ Check out the International Volunteer Programs Association (IVPA) at *www.volunteerinternational.org*. IVPA is an alliance of nonprofit organizations offering a great range of international volunteer and internship opportunities. For other reputable organizations doing good work around the world, turn to the Resources section.

THEME-ORIENTED TRAVEL

➤ Theme-oriented travel presents another good way to deepen and focus your experiences on the road. It allows you to connect travel to your passions or nurture a fledgling interest.

➤ Do you love to cook? Are you fascinated by Thailand? Why not attend a cooking school in Bangkok? Is the Maine coast your favorite place to vacation, and you've just picked up photography? The seaside village of Rockport hosts one of the most extensive photography programs in the country. Are you dying to learn Spanish, as well as tromp around for a few months with a backpack? Why not enroll in a language-immersion school in Quito, Ecuador? You'll be surprised by how quickly you learn the language in such an intensive context, and then you can explore South America with new communication skills.

➤ Consider what type of vacation you want when selecting your tour, trek, language program, holistic center, or painting workshop. Do you want something intensive or relaxed? Something solitary or with a group? Would you rather spend a weekend away or a month? As always, the clearer you are about your wants and needs, the wiser your choices will be.

➤ Create your own special itinerary. You don't necessarily need a tour, program, or school to explore your interests while traveling. Do a little research about the place you're going. Find out about the museums, wildlife, handicrafts or whatever it is that makes your heart soar, and build a trip around your passion.

XIX
PACKING

On a long journey even a straw weighs heavy.
—*Spanish Proverb*

———

BEFORE EVERY TRIP I agonize about what to pack. Should I use my roll-aboard, a sturdy duffel bag, or a big suitcase? Which shoes, coats, clothing should I take? To reduce this stress I begin to tuck items into my bag days before departure. For a short trip, I might pack one or two days in advance. For an adventure trip, such as trekking in the Himalayas, I begin checking my gear (hiking boots, fanny pack, warm coats, flashlights, etc.) weeks before.

Recently I packed in two days for a two-week trip—camping in the Sahara Desert, exploring Morocco's Atlas Mountains, Roman ruins, and imperial cities. How? The adventure travel company who operated the trip sent me a comprehensive packing list. All my gear fit into one duffel bag, and, surprisingly, I didn't have to buy any new clothes or equipment.

I like lists. They keep me organized. I keep several versions in my luggage and highlight in bright yellow the items I continually forget, such as dental floss, belts, and fresh batteries for flashlights. My goal is to pack so efficiently that when I unpack after a trip I discover I have worn or used every item in my bag.

TIPS

➤ When in doubt, leave it out—a good packing motto to help remind you to pack lightly.

➤ Pack doubles of anything you *really* can't live without, like your contact lenses, prescription sunglasses, a copy of your passport, driver's license, or credit card. I even pack two tubes of lip balm and stuff my empty shoes with feminine hygiene supplies.

➤ Pack space-consciously. Roll everything (business suits, blazers, etc.); use dry cleaners' plastic bags between clothing; bring wrinkle-free skirts or pants.

➤ Keep all your luggage organized. Bring zip-lock bags with you. One week into your trip, you'll wish you had brought more. They keep freshly washed but not-quite-dry underwear separated from dry clothes, pills and vitamins separate from snacks. These see-through bags, available in all sizes make it easy to find everything from tampons to batteries to flashlights.

➤ Pack comfy walking shoes! Your shoes must be well worn in before you leave on the trip. Pack extra socks that dry quickly and wick the moisture away from your feet. Bring moleskin in case you develop blisters. Also consider bringing talcum powder to sprinkle in your shoes if you will be walking a lot. This prevents rashes and sweaty feet in hot climates. Wear your bulkiest, heaviest pair of shoes or hiking boots on the plane.

➤ Bring one quick-drying travel outfit. Cotton, wool, and linen clothing is impractical, heavy, and outdated for your travel wardrobe. Get with it! New travelwear for women combines practical design with performance fabric. Quick-drying fabrics

---

_____ ⚡ _____

Some women make a fetish of preparing for a trip. I'm a last-minute packer. I figure if I've got my airline ticket, passport if necessary, and a couple of credit cards, any forgotten object can always be replaced.

◆

Claire Walter, editor/travel writer, Boulder, Colorado

_____ ⚡ _____

Clothes wrinkle less in a garment bag if you hang them in the plastic covering from the dry cleaners. Plastic bags from the vegetable department of the supermarket are perfect for shoes.

◆

Laurie Armstrong, 37, vice president, San Francisco Convention and Visitors Bureau

enable on-the-road wash and wear, while others even remove moisture from your body. This type of fabric is designed for wear on sea-kayaking trips, alpine treks, rafting adventures, and any other activity where you may get wet but must stay dry and warm. Always dress in layers. Shop from a specialized travel catalog or store and splurge on a pair of travel pants (some available with zip-off shorts) and a long-sleeve travel shirt.

➤ Invest in an all-weather travel coat. Although your choice will depend upon the climate of your destination and your adventure activities, a rainproof all-weather coat is essential. It should be light, have many pockets, and feature a hood.

➤ Wear layers of clothing if you are going to a place where the climate changes dramatically from day to night or if you plan lots of outdoor activities.

➤ Always pack your bathing suit. You never know when you'll have an opportunity to swim or hop in a hot tub, and there is no better tension reliever.

➤ Instead of packing a nightgown or pajamas I bring a large t-shirt. It doubles as a cover-up for the beach or pool and I can give it away at the end of the trip.

➤ Adventure gear is different than conventional luggage. The type of principal luggage you will need depends on the type of travel you do. It may accompany you through the streets of Paris or Florence or be tied to the back of a yak or pack animal in the Andes or Himalayas. All destinations, after all, are not alike and your packing needs from trip to trip will

—— ⚶ ——

I never travel without a sarong. Sometimes it can be a skirt, a dress, a beach cover-up, a belt, a carry-all, a bathrobe, or a tablecloth. It is so versatile.

◆

Christine Wilson, 50, outdoor adventurer, guide, and volunteer, Portland, Oregon

most likely vary. Decide what kind of traveler you are: sports and recreation, wilderness, urban, independent or traditional, then research your options.

Your travel pack will also have to fit under your seat or in the overhead bin on a plane, in the baggage compartment of a bus, or on the overhead shelf on a train.

➤ What to pack? If you are going on an organized tour, the tour company should provide you with a complete packing list tailored to your destination, its climate, and your activities. If you are traveling on your own, the packing list in the Resources section can become your own master list. Xerox the list and use it for future trips.

One of the smartest things I ever did was have my colors done—not because I'm fashion-conscious, but because dressing in my "palette" allows me to pack light and still look coordinated. From one carry-on bag I can dress for just about any occasion.

♦

Glenda Winders, 50, editorial manager, Copley News Service, San Diego, California

➤ Throw out the hard suitcase. It belongs to the era of the carry-on cosmetic kit. Try a roll-aboard that will fit under the seat or in the overhead. If a roll-aboard isn't for you, try a sturdy duffel bag with built-in compartments. Shop for these in a store specializing in travel luggage.

➤ When buying a travel pack, consider the bag's durability—how much abuse can it take? Look for beefy zippers and finished seams. For the sake of your shoulders, arms, and hands, look for comfy handles and straps.

PACKING FOR THE PLANE

➤ Carry all your medications with you on the plane, in case your checked luggage gets lost or delayed.

➤ My list of items to take on the plane includes reading materials, earplugs, eye shields, neck pillow, socks, a sweater, several nutritious snacks (green apple, granola bar, dried fruit), a full water bottle, Chapstick, toothbrush and toothpaste, extra glasses, contact lens kit, pens, stationery, address book, and a calculator.

➤ Conquer cold feet. The temperature on airplanes can vary from tropical heat to arctic chill during a flight and you can't count on finding an airline blanket when you need it. Dress in layers, bring a sweater, and pack slipper-socks in your carry-on bag.

> ＿＿ ⚜ ＿＿
>
> You may have to fly first or business class to get those soft, dark "airplane" socks to slip on when you shuck your cordovans on long flights. But it's easier to bring your own. Throw a pair of oversize hiking socks into your carry-on bag.
>
> ◆
>
> *Judy Wade, 50,*
> *travel writer/photographer,*
> *Phoenix, Arizona*

Take them out before you stash it overhead or under the seat.

➤ The air circulated in airplane cabins is extremely dry. When traveling by plane, carry lip balm and moisturizer to prevent chapped lips.

➤ Earplugs to the rescue. Inexpensive silicon earplugs reduce the noise on airplanes to help you concentrate on work or reading a good novel. They also regulate the flow of air into your ears and allow you to adapt better to pressure changes. Available at drugstores or airport shops, silicon earplugs (not foam) work the best.

➤ When I pack, I include in my carry-on bag all of my old, unread magazines and my favorite sections of the most recent Sunday *New York Times*. As I read them, I discard them or give them to expatriates or other Americans, who always seem to appreciate my cast-off reading material.

➤ No nylons aboard. Recent tests have shown that when women

slide down an airplane's emergency escape ramp, the friction and heat generated from the slide melted their nylon stockings to their legs. Chances are you'll never have to exit a plane this way, but just in case, don't wear pantyhose when you fly.

➤ Identify your bags. More and more people are traveling with black roll-aboard suitcases. Twice someone has mistakenly grabbed my roll-aboard off the baggage-claim carousel. To avoid problems, identify your luggage with something colorful, such as yellow or red ID tags, tie a ribbon around the handle, or wrap a guitar strap around the suitcase.

➤ Provide minimal information on baggage identification tags. I list only my first initial, last name, and geographic area: M. Bond, San Francisco, California. If my bags are lost, airline personnel can locate me through the computer. The information I have provided is too vague for anyone to find my residence, phone number, profession, or place of employment.

➤ Identification tags are often torn off during baggage handling. Be sure to have full identification inside your luggage.

PACKING ESSENTIALS

➤ Put your money in a money belt. You've worked for it. You've saved it. Now protect it and enjoy spending it! Buy a money belt or pouch and wear your valuables close to your heart (or torso). Keep credit cards, travelers' checks, passport, and large bills in it. How much money to bring? Take 20 percent more than you think you'll need. Don't forget to take about twenty one-dollar bills for tips.

➤ Pack a first-aid kit. Don't forget pills, bandages, Imodium, an ample supply of Pepto Bismol and Alka Seltzer tablets, tampons, antibacterial gel, sunscreen, lip balm, and mosquito repellent. Another must is an all-purpose antibiotic, such as Ciproflaxacin, which can be used for serious traveler's diarrhea, upper respiratory problems, and more. A prescription is necessary, so consult with your doctor.

➤ Emergen-C—many experienced travelers won't leave home without this dietary supplement. Those powdered vitamin C packets, available at health food stores, are essential in any tropical climate because they replace electrolytes and fluids lost through perspiration. If you have treated your water with iodine, it will improve the taste.

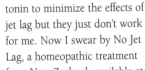

I've tried special diets and melatonin to minimize the effects of jet lag but they just don't work for me. Now I swear by No Jet Lag, a homeopathic treatment from New Zealand, available at specialized travel stores as well as Magellan's and Trader Joe's. I won't travel overseas without it.

◆

MBB

➤ Bring a small bottle of antibacterial gel. Then you can always wash your hands before meals and after pit stops.

➤ A Swiss Army knife is an indispensable travel tool. Be sure to travel with a model that includes a pair of tweezers, scissors, a corkscrew, and a toothpick. Pack it in your checked luggage.

➤ Duct tape to the rescue. Have you ever had a sandal strap break or the handle fall off your suitcase mid-trip? Pack a long strip of duct tape for unexpected repairs. Just wrap it around a pen and tuck it in your bag.

➤ Shampoo—from hair to hosiery. If you're staying in relatively nice hotels, don't bother to pack washing detergent. The shampoo provided by your hotel can be used to wash out underwear or hosiery.

➤ If you're traveling on a budget and your hotels are unlikely to provide shampoo, pack a Zip-lock bag full of detergent for washing your clothes.

➤ Save your eyes. Do you find that your eyes ache or feel tired when you read in your hotel room? Guess what—many hotels provide only 60- to 90-watt lightbulbs in the lamp. So pack a 100- to 150-watt lightbulb to work or read in your room and ease your eyes. Or call ahead and ask that 100-watt lightbulbs be installed in your room before you arrive.

➤ Avoid camera calamities. Carry lots of extra film, because it's very expensive abroad. Also pack extra batteries for your cameras. If, by accident, you leave the shutter open or flash on overnight, your battery will be dead in the morning. You may not find the size and brand of battery you need easily.

➤ Pack a drain stopper. Travel nuts know how important a drain stopper can be! How else can you take a bath or plug up the sink to wash clothes, if the place you're staying doesn't have one? The flat type are best to cover a variety of sink drains and are available at hardware stores.

➤ Pack an extra nylon duffel inside your luggage to store items in a hotel in the event you travel to other cities and want to leave a bag behind. It is also useful as an extra piece of luggage to carry home purchases.

➤ Take along photos of your home, pets, and family as well as colorful postcards of your hometown. Postcards are easy gifts, and personal photos help you share your world. A frisbee, puppet, or colored pens and pencils will win you friends.

➤ Pack positive, inspiring books that you can trade with other travelers. Look for women's travel narratives.

➤ Pack a sense of humor, no matter what else you bring.

The first things into my suitcase are always the bandannas—at least a half-dozen per trip, in a variety of bright colors. Nothing so light, so easy to pack, has ever played so many roles, saved so many days. The simple cotton squares serve as headbands when hiking; cooling, damp neckerchiefs when worn wet in a steamy jungle; fast-drying washcloths in all those hotels and hostels that don't provide them; or washcloths in camp that can be quick-dipped in a stream and quick-dried, draped over a branch or bush. They are often the only end-of-the-day solution to "hat head" or wilted beach hair, a plague I am prone to even in the desert. Thus, my bandannas go wherever my passport goes. And, invariably, I give the lavenders and yellows and tie-dyes away along the way, coming home even lighter than I left.

♦

Paula McDonald, 50+, author and photojournalist, Baja California, Mexico

XX
THE FINAL WORD

Through travel I first became aware of the outside world; it was through travel that I found my own introspective way into becoming a part of it.

—*Eudora Welty*

"HOW HAS TRAVEL CHANGED YOUR LIFE?" someone once asked me in an interview. Travel has changed me in many ways. It's made me more aware of the world around me. It's brought extraordinary people into my life. It's taught me to give up control. It's deepened my sense of awe. In answering the question, though, I realized the single most important way travel has affected me: It's made me deeply comfortable with *myself*. Before I traveled around the world at age twenty-nine, I had never gone to a movie or out to eat alone. On airplanes I was so scared I took sleeping pills. Now, after years of travel and risk taking, I savor the moments I have to myself. I have learned to listen deeply to myself, and to have confidence in my choices. I am a Gutsy Woman.

Gutsy does not mean fearless. On the contrary—it means coming close enough to our fears that we realize the depth of our courage.

And through travel, we come to know and summon that courage. For as we leave our well-trod terrain and all that is familiar behind, we leave our comfort zones. Whether communicating in a new language, finding our way alone through a foreign city, or tasting strange new food, travel challenges and stretches us. As we test ourselves, we break through limiting ideas of ourselves. We discover that we are more than what we thought; we can do more than we imagined. We can break with tradition, try on new roles, cross boundaries imposed by society or the routines of our day-to-day lives. As we travel, we reclaim our sense of self and strength. Travel takes us to the core of ourselves, and it changes us.

My hope, thus, is that the tips, wisdom, and personal anecdotes presented in this second edition of *Gutsy Women* will help inform and illuminate your own unique path—the one that draws you boldly out into the world and inevitably, bravely, into yourself. I hope that the voices of the many women quoted in this book have inspired you to crack open your own fears and discover the treasures within.

So be a Gutsy Woman—you know you already are! Take a trip—it doesn't matter if it's a monthlong trek in the Himalayas or a day-long excursion to a local beach. What's important is trying something new, something compelling and maybe even a little scary. Something you've dreamed about. Whatever it is, try it. See how it feels. See what you learn about yourself. It may be something you never imagined. Something wonderful. Something surprising. Something...*gutsy*.

XXI
RESOURCES AND REFERENCES

BOOKS, MAGAZINES, AND
NEWSLETTERS

Reading—both preparing for my adventure and reading on the trip—is a great part of the pleasure of travel for me. I look forward to having time to read when I travel. I read in the airporter bus; while I wait in airports; on flights, buses, and trains; in restaurants; and even, when there is no electricity, by flashlight in bed.

Anthologies and Travelogues

Ackerman, Diane. *A Natural History of the Senses*. New York: Vintage Books, 1991.

Aebi, Tania, with Bernadette Brennan. *Maiden Voyage*. New York: Ballantine Publishing Group, 1996.

Bird, Isabella L. *A Lady in the Rocky Mountains*. Norman: The University of Oklahoma Press, 1999.

Bird, Isabella L. *Unbeaten Tracks of Japan*. San Francisco: Travelers' Tales, 2000.

Blum, Arlene. *Annapurna: A Woman's Place*. San Francisco: Sierra Club Books, 1998.

Bolen, Jean. *Crossing to Avalon*. San Francisco: HarperSanFrancisco, 1994.

Bond, Marybeth, and Pamela Michael, eds. *A Mother's World: Journeys of the Heart*. San Francisco: Travelers' Tales, 1998.

Bond, Marybeth, and Pamela Michael, eds. *A Woman's Passion for Travel: More True Stories from a Woman's World*. San Francisco: Travelers' Tales, 1999.

Bond, Marybeth, ed. *Travelers' Tales: A Woman's World*. San Francisco: Travelers' Tales, 1995.

da Silva, Rachel. *Leading Out: Mountaineering Stories of Adventurous Women*. Seattle: Seal Press, 1998.

David-Neel, Alexandra. *My Journey to Lhasa*. Boston: Beacon Press, 1993.

Davidson, Robyn. *Tracks: A Woman's Solo Trek across 1,700 Miles of Australian Outback*. New York: Random House, 1980.

Fisher, M. F. K. *Two Towns in Provence: Map of Another Town and a Considerable Town*. New York: Vintage, 1994.

Geniesse, Jane Fletcher. *Passionate Nomad: The Life of Freya Stark*. New York: Random House, 1999.

Goldberg, Natalie. *Long Quiet Highway: Waking Up in America*. New York: Bantam, 1994.

Gosnell, Mariana. *Zero Three Bravo: Solo across America in a Small Plane*. New York: Touchstone Books, 1994.

Gough, Laurie. *Kite Strings of the Southern Cross: A Woman's Travel Odyssey*. San Francisco: Travelers' Tales, 2000.

Hadley, Leila. *Give Me the World*. New York: Thomas Dunne Books, 1999.

Holmes-Binney, Debi. *Desert Sojourn: A Woman's Forty Days and Nights Alone*. Seattle: Seal Press, 2000.

Johnston, Tracy. *Shooting the Boh: A Woman's Voyage down the Wildest River in Borneo*. New York: Random House, 1992.

Lee, Elaine, ed. *Go Girl: The Black Woman's Guide to Travel and Adventure*. Portland: Eighth Mountain Press, 1997.

Manske, Laura. *Family Travel: The Farther You Go the Closer You Get*. San Francisco: Travelers' Tales, 1999.

Markham, Beryl. *West with the Night*. New York: North Point Press, 1985.

Mayes, Frances. *Under the Tuscan Sun: At Home in Italy*. New York: Broadway Books, 1997.

McCauley, Lucy, ed. *Women in the Wild: True Stories of Adventure and Connection*. San Francisco: Travelers' Tales, 1998.

McCauley, Lucy, Amy G. Carlson, and Jennifer Leo, eds. *A Woman's Path: Women's Best Spiritual Writing*. San Francisco: Travelers' Tales, 2000.

Morris, Mary, and Larry O'Connor, eds. *Maiden Voyages: Writings of Women Travelers*. New York: Vintage Departures, 1993.

Morris, Mary. *Nothing to Declare: Memoirs of a Woman Traveling Alone*. New York: Houghton Mifflin Company, 1988.

Morrow, Susan Brind. *The Names of Things: Life, Language, and Beginnings in the Egyptian Desert*. New York: Riverhead Books, 1998.

Murphy, Dervla. *South from the Limpopo: Travels Through South Africa*. Woodstock, NY: Overlook, Press, 2000.

Norris, Kathleen. *Dakota: A Spiritual Geography*. New York: Houghton Mifflin, 1994.

Owens, Mark and Delia. *Cry of the Kalahari*. New York: Houghton Mifflin, 1992.

Rogers, Susan Fox, ed. *Another Wilderness: New Outdoor Writing by Women*. Seattle: Seal Press, 1994.

Rogers, Susan Fox, ed. *Solo: On Her Own Adventure*. Seattle: Seal Press, 1996.

Savage, Barbara. *Miles from Nowhere: A Round-the-World Bicycle Adventure*. Seattle: The Mountaineers, 1988.

Stark, Freya. *Baghdad Sketches*. New York: Marlboro Press, 1996.

Steinbach, Alice. *Without Reservations: The Travels of an Independent Woman*. New York: Random House, 2000.

Thayer, Helen. *Polar Dream: The Heroic Saga of the First Solo Journey by a Woman and Her Dog to the Pole*. New York: Simon and Schuster, Inc., 1993.

Williams, Terry Tempest. *Refuge: An Unnatural History of Family and Place*. New York: Vintage Books, 1992.

Zeppa, Jamie. *Beyond the Sky and the Earth: A Journey into Bhutan*. New York: Riverhead Books, 1999.

Resource Books

Borrus, Kathy. *The Fearless Shopper: How to Get the Best Deals on the Planet*. San Francisco: Travelers' Tales, 1999.

Fodor's Great American Learning Vacations: Hundreds of Workshops, Camps, and Tours That Will Satisfy Your Curiosity and Enrich Your Life. New York: Fodor's Travel Publications, Inc., 1997.

Gilford, Judith. *The Packing Book: Secrets of the Carry-On Traveler*. Berkeley: Ten Speed Press, 1998.

Jansz, Natania, Miranda Davies, Emma Drew, and Lori McDougall, eds. *Women Travel: A Rough Guide Special*. London: Rough Guides, 1999.

McMillon, Bill. *Volunteer Vacations: A Directory of Short Term Adventures That Will Benefit You and Others*. Chicago: Chicago Review Press, 1999.

Schnedler, Marcia. *The Seasoned Traveler*. Castine, Maine: Country Roads Press, 1992.

Schroeder, Dirk. *Staying Healthy in Asia, Africa, and Latin America*. Emeryville, Calif.: Avalon Publications, 2000.

Shapiro, Michael. *Internet Travel Planner*. Connecticut: Globe Pequot Press, 2000.

Sterling, Richard. *The Fearless Diner*. San Francisco: Travelers' Tales, 1998.

Swan, Sheila, and Peter Laufer. *Safety and Security for Women Who Travel*. San Francisco: Travelers' Tales, 1998.

Widzer, Joel. *The Penny Pincher's Passport to Luxury Travel: The Art of Cultivating Preferred Customer Status*. San Francisco: Travelers' Tales, 1999.

Wilson-Howarth, Jane. *Shitting Pretty: How to Stay Clean and Healthy While Traveling*. San Francisco: Travelers' Tales, 2000.

Zepatos, Thalia. *Adventures in Good Company: The Complete Guide to Women's Tours & Outdoor Trips*. Portland: Eighth Mountain Press, 1994.

Zobel, Louise Purwin. *The Travel Writer's Handbook*. Chicago: Surrey Books, 1997.

Travel Newsletters and Magazines

Newsletters and magazines focusing on travel can be found in both traditional print as well as online. A visit to your local newstand or bookstore and an afternoon surfing the Web will yield a large variety to choose from. Narrow your selection to those publications which suit your destination or travel style. Start by checking out the following:

Backpacker
Blue
Condé Nast Traveler
Connecting—Solo Travel News
Islands
Journeywoman
National Geographic Traveler
Outside
Passionfruit
Transitions Abroad
Travel-Holiday
Travel Matters
Trips
Wanderlust

SERVICES AND ORGANIZATIONS

Tour Services

Above the Clouds Trekking
P.O. Box 388
Hinesburg, VT 05461
800-233-4499 or 802-482-4848
www.aboveclouds.com

Adventure Divas
2328 E. Madison
Seattle, WA 98112
206-328-9519
www.adventuredivas.com

Adventures in Good Company
5506 Trading Post Trail
Afton, MN 55001
877-439-4042 or 651-998-0120
www.goodadventure.com

Adventure Women, Inc.
15033 Kelly Canyon Road
Bozeman, MT 59715
800-804-8686 or 406-587-3883
www.adventurewomen.com

Asia Transpacific Journeys
2995 Center Green Court
Boulder, CO 80301
800-642-2742 or 303-443-6789
www.southeastasia.com

Backcountry
P.O. Box 4029
Bozeman, MT 59772
800-575-1540 or 406-586-3556
www.backcountrytours.com

Backroads
801 Cedar Street
Berkeley, CA 94710-1800
800-462-2848 or 510-527-1555
www.backroads.com

Becoming an Outdoors Woman
College of Natural Resources
University of Wisconsin, Stevens Point
Stevens Point, WI 54481-3897
877-269-6626 or 715-346-4151
www.uwsp.edu/bow

Call of the Wild
2519 Cedar Street
Berkeley, CA 94708
510-849-9292
www.callwild.com

Fifth World Pilgrimages
785 32nd Street
Boulder, CO 80303
877-556-1519 or 720-406-9151
www.fifthworld.com

Gearhead
4835 North O'Connor Road, Suite 134-338
Irving, TX 75062
888-443-2743
www.thegearhead.com

Going Places
P.O. Box 2034
Sonoma, CA 95476
707-935-0595
www.goingplaces.com

Hawk, I'm Your Sister
P.O. Box 9109
Santa Fe, NM 87504-9109
505-984-2268
www.womansplace.com

Inca Floats
1311 63rd Street
Emeryville, CA 94608
510-420-1550
www.incafloats.com

International Expeditions
One Environs Park
Helena, AL 35080

800-633-4734
www.ietravel.com

Journeys
107 Aprill Drive, Suite 3
Ann Arbor, MI 48103
800-255-8735 or 734-665-4407

Mariah Wilderness Expeditions
P.O. Box 70248
Point Richmond, CA 94807
510-233-2303
www.mariahwe.com

Maupin Tours
1421 Research Park Dr. Suite 300
Lawrence, KS 66049-3858
800-255-4266
www.maupintours.com

Mountain Travel/Sobek
6420 Fairmount Avenue
El Cerrito, CA 94530-3606
888-MTSOBEK or 510-527-8100
www.mtsobek.com

Myths and Mountains
976 Tee Court
Incline Village, NV 89451
800-670-6984 or 775-832-5454
www.mythsandmountains.com

Natural Habitat Adventures
2945 Center Green Court, Suite H
Boulder, CO 80301

800-543-8917 or 303-449-3711
www.nathab.com

Nature Expeditions International
6400 East El Dorado Circle, Suite 210
Tucson, AZ 85715
800-869-0639 or 954-693-8852
www.naturexp.com

Sacred Journeys for Women
P.O. Box 893
Occidental, CA 95465
888-779-6696 or 707-524-4030
www.sacredjourneys.com

Sheri Griffith Expeditions
P.O. Box 1324
Moab, UT 84532
800-332-2439
www.griffithexp.com

Thomson Safaris and Thomson Family Adventures
347 Broadway
Cambridge, MA 02139
800-235-0289 or 617-876-7314
www.thomsonsafaris.com
www.familyadventures.com

Turtle Tours, Inc.
Box 1147/Dept. ES
Carefree, AZ 85377
888-299-1439 or 480-488-3688

Wild Women Adventures
152 Bloomfield Road
Sebastopol, CA 95472

800-992-1322 or 707-829-3670
www.wildwomenadv.com

Wilderness Travel
1102 9th Street
Berkeley, CA 94710
800-368-2794 or 510-558-2488
www.wildernesstravel.com

Womanship
137 Conduit Street
Annapolis, MD 21401
800-342-9295 or 410-267-6661
www.womanship.com

The Women's Travel Club
21401 N.E. 38th Avenue
Aventura, FL 33180
800-480-4448 or 305-936-9669
www.womenstravelclub.com

Lesbian Travel

Above and Beyond Tours
230 N. Via Las Palmas
Palm Springs, CA 92262
800-397-2681 or 760-325-1702
www.abovebeyondtours.com

Alyson Adventures, Inc.
P.O. Box 180179
Boston, MA 02118
800-8-ALYSON or 617-542-1177
www.alysonadventures.com

Gay and Lesbian Travel Specialists Network
2300 Market Street, Suite #142

San Francisco, CA 94114
415-552-5140

In the Company of Women
Box 522344
Longwood, FL 32752
407-331-3466
www.companyofwomen.com

International Gay Travel Association
4331 North Federal Highway, Suite 304
Fort Lauderdale, FL 33308
800-448-8550 or 954-776-2626

Left Coast Travel/Gay and Lesbian Travel Specialists
1655 Polk Street, Suite 1
San Francisco, CA 94109
800-TAD-LEFT or 415-771-5353

Olivia Tours & Cruises
4400 Market Street
Oakland, CA 94608
800-631-6277 or 510-655-0364
www.oliviatravel.com

VentureOut
575 Pierce Street, #604
San Francisco, CA 94117
888-431-6789 or 415-626-5678
www.venture-out.com

Mature/Senior Travel

Elderhostel
75 Federal Street
Boston, MA 02110

877-426-7788 or 617-426-7788
www.elderhostel.org

Eldertreks
597 Markham Street
Toronto, Ontario, Canada M6G 2L7
800-741-7956 or 416-588-5000
www.eldertreks.com

Explorations in Travel, Inc.
1922 River Road
Guilford, VT 05301
802-257-0152
www.exploretravel.com

Folkways Travel
14600 SE Aldridge Road
Portland, OR 97236-6518
800-225-4666 or 503-658-6600
folkwaystrvl@aol.com

Grand Circle Travel
347 Congress Street
Boston, MA 02210
800-859-0852
www.gct.com

Interhostel
University of New Hampshire
6 Garrison Avenue
Durham, NH 03824
800-733-9753 or 603-862-4471
www.learn.unh.edu/INTERHOSTEL

Overseas Adventure Travel
347 Congress Street

Boston, MA 02210
800-221-0814 or 617-350-7500
www.gct.com

Saga International Holidays
222 Berkeley Street
Boston, MA 02116
800-343-0273
www.sagaholidays.com

Senior Women's Travel
Stanton Associates
136 East 56th Street
New York, NY 10022
212-838-4740
www.poshnosh.com

Walking the World
P.O. Box 1186
Fort Collins, CO 80522
800-340-9255 or 970-498-0500
www.walkingtheworld.com

Volunteer Opportunities

Cross-Cultural Solutions (CCS)
47 Potter Avenue
New Rochelle, NY 10801
800-380-4777 or 914-632-0022
www.crossculturalsolutions.org

Earthwatch
3 Clocktower Place, Suite 100
Box 75
Maynard, MA 01754
800-776-0188 or 978-461-0081
www.earthwatch.org

Global Exchange
2017 Mission Street #303
San Francisco, CA 94110
800-255-7296 or 415-255-7296
www.globalexchange.org

Global Service Corps
300 Broadway #28
San Francisco, CA 94133
415-788-3666
www.globalservicecorps.org

Global Volunteers
375 East Little Canada Road
St. Paul, MN 55117
800-487-1074 or 651-407-6100
www.globalvolunteers.org

Habitat for Humanity
322 West Lamar Street
Americus, GA 31709
800-422-4828 or 9120924-6935
www.habitat.org

International Volunteers Program Association
www.volunteerinternational.org

Mennonite Central Committee (MCC)
21 South 12th Street
Akron, PA 17501-0500
717-859-1151
www.mcc.org

New World Teachers
605 Market Street, Suite 750
San Francisco, CA 94105

800-644-5424 or 415-546-5200
www.goteach.com

Peace Brigades International
1904 Franklin Street, Suite 505
Oakland, CA 94612
510-663-2362
www.igc.org/pbi/usa.html

RSVP International
500 5th Avenue, 35th Floor
New York, NY 10110
212-575-1800

Volunteers in Asia (VIA)
Haas Center for Public Service
P.O. Box 4535
Stanford, CA 94309
650-723-3228
www.volasia.org

Worldteach
Harvard Institute for International Development
79 JFK Street
Cambridge, MA 02138-5705
800-4-TEACH-0 or 617-495-5527
www.worldteach.org

Homestays

American-International Homestays, Inc.
P.O. Box 1754
Nederland, CO 80466
800-876-2048 or 303-258-3234
www.aihtravel.com/homestays

The Experiment in International Living
High school, college, and graduate students

Kipling Road
P.O. Box 676
Brattleboro, VT 05301
800-345-2929 or 802-257-7751
www.usexperiment.org

Friendship Force
34 Peachtree Street, Suite 900
Atlanta, GA 30303
404-522-9490
www.friendship-force.org

LEX Exchange, LEX America
68 Leonard Street, Suite 9
Belmont, MA 02178
617-489-5800
www.petersons.com/summerop/sites

Servas International
11 John Street, Suite 407
New York, NY 10038
212-267-0252
www.usservas.org

World Learning
P.O. Box 676
Brattleboro, VT 05302
802-257-7751
www.worldlearning.org

Fear of Flying

Fearless Flyer Classes
American Airlines
1-800-451-5106

Freedom from Fear of Flying, Inc.
2021 Country Club Prado

Coral Gables, FL 33134
305-261-7042

Pegasus Fear of Flying Foundation
8 Horseshoe Trail
Barnardsvilles, NC 28709
1-800-FEAR-NOT or 828-626-3072
www.pegasus-fear-fly.com

WORLD WIDE WEB RESOURCES

There is a lot of information about women's travel on the Web.
Whether you're throwing around destination ideas, looking for
somewhere to stay, or searching for basic travel tips, the following
lists should be helpful. The Web has produced a wealth of general
women's sites, that are worth checking out.

Accommodations

The Hostel Handbook
www.hostelhandbook.com

Hostelling International
www.hiayh.org

Hostels.com
www.hostels.com/hostel.menu.htm

Landfair Home Exchange
www.landfair.com

Wildflower Travel Community
www.escape.ca/~livana

Women's Travel Reservation Network
www.womenstravel.co.nz

WorldHotel
www.escope.com/trl.html

Sites for Women on the Net

Cybergrrl
www.cybergrrl.com

Fabula
www.fabulamag.com

Femina
http://femina.cybergrrl.com

Feminist.com
www.feminist.com

Girls Internationally Writing Letters
http://carol.tierranet.com/old/girlpage.htm

Grand Style Women's Club
www.grandstyle.com

iVillage.com
www.ivillage.com

Pleiades Network
www.pleiades-net.com

Women's International Network News
www.feminist.com/win.htm

WomensNet
www.igc.org/igc/gateway/wnindex.html

WWWomen Webring
www.wwwomen.com

Women's Wire
www.womenswire.com

Web Sites Specific to Women's Travel

Adventure Divas
www.adventuredivas.com

Fifty Plus One
www.interguru.com/fiftyplusone

Journeywoman
www.journeywoman.com

Maiden Voyages
http://maiden-voyages.com

Marybeth Bond
www.marybethbond.com

Rec. Travel Library
www.travel-library.com

Sally's Place
www.sallys-place.com

Totally Outdoors
www.totallyoutdoors.com

Women-networking.com
www.women-networking.com/weekendpassport

Women Traveling Together
www.women-traveling.com

Women Welcome Women
www.womenwelcomewomen.org

I also recommend searching under the categories: *Languages, Health, Currency, Transportation, Statistics, Demographics,* and *Security*.

MISCELLANEOUS RESOURCES

Credit Card Advice

American Express
800-528-4800 in the U.S.
623-492-8596 collect from abroad

Diner's Club
800-346-3779 in the U.S.
702-797-5532 collect from abroad

Discover
800-347-2683
(Discover is not accepted outside the U.S.)

MasterCard
800-622-7747 in the U.S.
314-542-7111 collect from abroad

Visa
800-336-8472 in the U.S.
410-581-9994 collect from abroad

Traveler's Check Advice

American Express
800-221-7282

Bank of America
800-227-6811
44-17-33-318-949 collect from abroad

Citicorp
800-645-6556 in the U.S.
813-623-1709 collect from abroad

Thomas Cook MasterCard
800-223-7373 in the U.S.
44-17-33-318-950 collect from abroad

Visa
800-227-6811 or 800-732-1322 in the U.S.
44-17-33-318-949 collect from abroad

Packing List

CLOTHING

___ belts
___ blouses
___ bras
___ boots
___ coats
___ dresses
___ gloves
___ hats
___ jackets
___ jeans
___ long t-shirt
___ panties
___ pantyhose
___ rain/sun hat
___ raincoat
___ scarves
___ shirts
___ shoes, dress
___ shoes, walking
___ shorts
___ skirts
___ slacks
___ slippers
___ socks
___ suits
___ sweat suit
___ sweaters
___ swimsuits

HYGIENE

___ body cream
___ brush/comb
___ dental floss
___ deodorant
___ face soap
___ foot powder
___ Kleenex
___ lip balm
___ magnifying
    mirror
___ makeup
___ moleskin
___ nail brush
___ nail clippers
___ nail file
___ nail polish
    remover
___ razor/blades
___ shampoo/con-
    ditioner
___ sunblock
___ surgical face
    mask
    or kerchief
___ tampons
___ toothbrush
___ toothpaste
___ tweezers

MEDICAL

___ antihistamines
___ antibiotic
    ointment
___ antiseptic skin
    cleanser
___ Band-aids
___ birth control
___ contact lenses
    and supplies
___ cotton swabs
___ diarrhea
    medicine
___ insect repellent
___ motion sickness
    remedy
___ muscle relaxant
___ nasal spray
___ Pepto Bismol/
    Alka Seltzer
___ prescription
    glasses (extra
    pair and copy
    of prescription
___ prescription
    medications
___ sleeping pills
___ Sting Stop™ gel
___ thermometer

DOCUMENTS

___ address book
___ credit cards
___ driver's license
___ family pictures
    (in plastic
    cover)
___ maps
___ passport/visas
___ passport photos
    (include extras)
___ photocopies of
    passport/visas
___ student ID card
___ travel insurance
___ travel tickets
___ travelers'
    checks

MISCELLANEOUS

___ alarm clock
___ batteries
___ calculator
___ camera/film
___ cash
___ clothesline
___ corkscrew
___ earplugs
___ electrical
    converter &
    adapter plugs
___ eyeshades
___ filmshield
___ flashlight
___ games/
    playing cards
___ guidebooks
___ highlighter pen
    (to mark maps)
___ journal
___ laundry deter-
    gent/Woolite
___ luggage locks
    (combination)
___ luggage tags
___ pens/pencils
___ phrase book
___ pillowcase
    (doubles as
    laundry bag)
___ pocket
    calculator
___ reading material

___ rubber bands
___ rubber door
    stopper
___ safety pins
___ scissors
___ sewing kit
___ stationery
___ sunglasses
___ tape recorder
    & tapes
___ watch
___ water bottle
___ whistle
___ zip-lock bags

Index of Contributors

Acknowledgments

I have been tolerated and my absences in mind and body forgiven by my patient, loving husband Gary and my heart's great joy, my daughters Julieclaire and Annalyse.

Two decades of my own travel experiences and a broad wealth of other travelers' wisdom have gone into the making of *Gutsy Women*. I couldn't have completed this book without help.

My heartfelt thanks to two talented writers and editors: Lisa Bach and Natanya Pearlman. They created structure from chaos and added wit, wisdom, thoughtful editing, and eloquent text to this book. They shared their writing expertise, insights, and humor with me. We share a mission and believe passionately in empowering and inspiring women to travel.

My heartfelt thanks to those who also helped with *Gutsy Women*: James O'Reilly, Larry Habegger, Wenda O'Reilly, Sean O'Reilly, Susan Brady, Deborah Greco, Jennifer Leo, Michelle Snider, Molly Thomas, and Tara Weaver at Travelers' Tales.

Simply, sincerely, thank you to all of my travel buddies, writer colleagues, supportive friends, mentors, and role models who have inspired, advised, and encouraged me: Alison DaRosa, Susan Spano, Lynn Ferrin, Alison Wright, Lisa Alpine, Carol Jacobs, Kari Bodnarchuk, Kim Brown, Laura Bly, Virginia Brownback, Janet Fullwood, Pamela Michael, Judy Wade, Olga Murray, Laurie Armstrong, Sarah Reyna, Carol Rivendell, Martha Lindt, and Susan Eckert.

About the Author

Marybeth Bond has not always been a Gutsy Woman. At summer camp, when she was ten years old, she was nicknamed "Misty" because she had a bad case of homesickness. Not one of her counselors would have predicted a traveling future for her. However, several decades later, Marybeth has hiked, cycled, climbed, dived, and kayaked her way through more than seventy countries around the world, from the depths of the Flores Sea to the summit of Mount Kilimanjaro. She studied in Paris for four years, earned two degrees, and had a business career in marketing.

At twenty-nine, she took off again, this time to travel alone around the world. These two years of travel changed her life. She met her future husband, an American, in Kathmandu, Nepal, and she returned to begin a new career as a writer, consultant, and lecturer. Since then she has given lectures around the world at such venues as the Explorers Club and Asia Society in New York.

Marybeth's first book, *A Woman's World,* is a best-seller and won the Lowell Thomas Gold Medal for Best Travel Book from the Society of American Travel Writers Foundation. It is an eloquent collection of women's writing that paints a rich portrait of what it means to be a woman today. She also coedited *A Mother's World* and *A Woman's Passion for Travel,* anthologies of women's travel writing.

As a nationally recognized travel expert and media personality, Marybeth has appeared on CBS News, CNN, ABC, NBC, Fox TV, and NPR. Marybeth was the "Smart Traveler" radio host for the nationally syndicated Outside Radio Show and the travel expert/columnist for the Travel Channel on ivillage.com, the women's online network. She is currently the "Travel Expert" for CBS's *Evening Magazine*.

Marybeth has two children, a husband, and a dog and lives in Northern California. She travels as much as she can—with her children, her husband, girlfriends, mother, or alone.

TRAVELERS' TALES

THE SOUL OF TRAVEL

Footsteps Series

KITE STRINGS OF THE SOUTHERN CROSS

A Woman's Travel Odyssey
By Laurie Gough
ISBN 1-885-211-54-6
$14.95

"Gough's poetic and sensual string of tales richly evokes the unexpected rewards—and perils—of the traveler's life. A striking, moving debut." — *Salon.com*

ForeWord Silver Medal Winner
— Travel Book of the Year

THE SWORD OF HEAVEN

A Five Continent Odyssey to Save the World
By Mikkel Aaland
ISBN 1-885-211-44-9
$24.00 (cloth)

"Few books capture the soul of the road like *The Sword of Heaven*, a sharp-edged, beautifully rendered memoir that will inspire anyone."

—Phil Cousineau, author of *The Art of Pilgrimage*

STORM

A Motorcycle Journey of Love, Endurance, and Transformation
By Allen Noren
ISBN 1-885-211-45-7
$24.00 (cloth)

"Beautiful, tumultuous, deeply engaging, and very satisfying."

—Ted Simon, author of *Jupiter's Travels*

TAKE ME WITH YOU

A Round-the-World Journey to Invite a Stranger Home
By Brad Newsham
ISBN 1-885-211-51-1
$24.00 (cloth)

"Newsham is an ideal guide. His journey, at heart, is into humanity."

—Pico Iyer, author of *Video Night in Kathmandu*

THE WAY OF THE WANDERER

Discover Your Hidden Selves Through Travel
By David Yeadon
ISBN 1-885-211-60-0
$14.95

Experience transformation through travel with this delightful, illustrated collection by award-winning author David Yeadon.

Travelers' Tales Classics

THE ROYAL ROAD TO ROMANCE
By Richard Halliburton
ISBN 1-885-211-53-8
$14.95

"Laughing at hardships, dreaming of beauty, ardent for adventure, Halliburton has managed to sing into the pages of this glorious book his own exultant spirit of youth and freedom."
— *Chicago Post*

UNBEATEN TRACKS IN JAPAN
By Isabella L. Bird
ISBN 1-885-211-57-0
$14.95

Isabella Bird gained a reputation as one of the most adventurous women travelers of the 19th century with her unconventional journeys to Tibet, Canada, Korea, Turkey, Hawaii, and Japan. A fascinating read for anyone interested in women's travel, spirituality, and Asian culture.

Europe

GREECE
True Stories of Life on the Road
Edited by Larry Habegger, Sean O'Reilly & Brian Alexander
ISBN 1-885-211-52-X
$17.95

"This is the stuff memories can be duplicated from."
— *Foreign Service Journal*

IRELAND
True Stories of Life on the Emerald Isle
Edited by James O'Reilly, Larry Habegger & Sean O'Reilly
ISBN 1-885-211-46-5
$17.95

Discover the wonder of Ireland with Frank McCourt, Thomas Flanagan, Nuala O'Faolain, Rosemary Mahoney, Colm Tóibín, and many more.

FRANCE
True Stories of Life on the Road
Edited by James O'Reilly, Larry Habegger & Sean O'Reilly
ISBN 1-885-211-02-3
$17.95

The French passion for life bursts forth from every page of this invaluable guide, featuring stories by Peter Mayle, M.F.K. Fisher, Ina Caro, Jan Morris, Jon Krakauer and many more.

PARIS
True Stories of Life on the Road
Edited by James O'Reilly, Larry Habegger & Sean O'Reilly
ISBN 1-885-211-10-4
$17.95

"If Paris is the main dish, here is a rich and fascinating assortment of hors d'oeuvres."
— *Peter Mayle, author of A Year in Provence*

ITALY
True Stories of Life on the Road
Edited by Anne Calcagno
Introduction by Jan Morris
ISBN 1-885-211-16-3
$17.95

ForeWord Silver Medal Winner—
Travel Book of the Year

SPAIN
True Stories of Life on the Road
Edited by Lucy McCauley
ISBN 1-885-211-07-4
$17.95

"A superb, eclectic collection that reeks wonderfully of gazpacho and paella, and resonates with sounds of heel-clicking and flamenco singing."
— *Barnaby Conrad, author of Matador*

Asia/Pacific

AUSTRALIA
True Stories of
Life Down Under
Edited by Larry Habegger
ISBN 1-885-211-40-6
$17.95
Explore Australia with
authors Paul Theroux,
Robyn Davidson, Bruce
Chatwin, Pico Iyer, Tim
Cahill, and many more.

JAPAN
True Stories of
Life on the Road
Edited by Donald W.
George & Amy
Greimann Carlson
ISBN 1-885-211-04-X
$17.95
"Readers of this entertain-
ing anthology will be better
equipped to plot a rewarding course through
the marvelously bewildering, bewitching
cultural landscape of Japan." — *Time* (Asia)

INDIA
True Stories of
Life on the Road
Edited by James O'Reilly
& Larry Habegger
ISBN 1-885-211-01-5
$17.95
"The Travelers' Tales series
should become required
reading for anyone visiting
a foreign country." — *St. Petersburg Times*

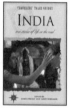

NEPAL
True Stories of
Life on the Road
Edited by Rajendra
S. Khadka
ISBN 1-885-211-14-7
$17.95
"If there's one thing tradi-
tional guidebooks lack, it's
the really juicy travel infor-
mation, the personal stories about back
alleys and brief encounters. This series fills
this gap." — *Diversion*

THAILAND
True Stories of
Life on the Road
Edited by James O'Reilly
& Larry Habegger
ISBN 1-885-211-05-8
$17.95

Winner of the Lowell
Thomas Award for Best
Travel Book — Society of
American Travel Writers

HONG KONG
True Stories of
Life on the Road
Edited by James O'Reilly,
Larry Habegger &
Sean O'Reilly
ISBN 1-885-211-03-1
$17.95
"Travelers' Tales Hong Kong
will delight the senses and
heighten the sensibilities, whether you are
an armchair traveler or an old China hand."
— *Profiles*

The Americas

AMERICA
True Stories of Life on the Road
Edited by Fred Setterberg
ISBN 1-885-211-28-7
$19.95

"Look no further.
This book is America."
—David Yeadon, author
of *Lost Worlds*

HAWAI'I
True Stories of the Island Spirit
Edited by Rick & Marcie Carroll
ISBN 1-885-211-35-X
$17.95

"Travelers' Tales aims to convey the excitement of voyaging through exotic territory with a vivacity that guidebooks can only hint at."—*Millenium Whole Earth Catalog*

GRAND CANYON
True Stories of Life Below the Rim
Edited by Sean O'Reilly, James O'Reilly & Larry Habegger
ISBN 1-885-211-34-1
$17.95

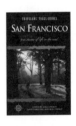

"Travelers' Tales should be required reading for anyone who wants to truly step off the tourist track."
— *St. Petersburg Times*

SAN FRANCISCO
True Stories of Life on the Road
Edited by James O'Reilly, Larry Habegger & Sean O'Reilly
ISBN 1-885-211-08-2
$17.95

"Like spying on the natives."
— *San Francisco Chronicle*

AMERICAN SOUTHWEST
True Stories
Edited by Sean O'Reilly and James O'Reilly
ISBN 1-885-211-58-9
$17.95

Put on your boots, saddle up, and explore the American Southwest with Terry Tempest Williams, Edward Abbey, Barbara Kingsolver, Alex Shoumatoff, and more.

BRAZIL
True Stories of Life on the Road
Edited by Annette Haddad & Scott Doggett
Introduction by Alex Shoumatoff
ISBN 1-885-211-11-2
$17.95

Benjamin Franklin Silver Award Winner

MEXICO
True Stories
Edited by James O'Reilly & Larry Habegger
ISBN 1-885-211-59-7
$17.95

— ★ ★ ★ —

One of the Year's Best Travel Books on Mexico
—**The New York Times**

Women's Travel

A WOMAN'S PASSION FOR TRAVEL
More True Stories from A Woman's World
Edited by Marybeth Bond & Pamela Michael
ISBN 1-885-211-36-8
$17.95

"A diverse and gripping series of stories!" —Arlene Blum, author of *Annapurna: A Woman's Place*

A WOMAN'S WORLD
True Stories of Life on the Road
Edited by Marybeth Bond
Introduction by Dervla Murphy
ISBN 1-885-211-06-6
$17.95

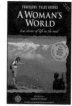

— ★ ★ ★ —

*Winner of the Lowell Thomas Award for Best Travel Book —
Society of American Travel Writers*

WOMEN IN THE WILD
True Stories of Adventure and Connection
Edited by Lucy McCauley
ISBN 1-885-211-21-X
$17.95

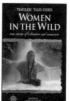

"A spiritual, moving, and totally female book to take you around the world and back." —*Mademoiselle*

A MOTHER'S WORLD
Journeys of the Heart
Edited by Marybeth Bond & Pamela Michael
ISBN 1-885-211-26-0
$14.95

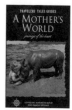

"These stories remind us that motherhood is one of the great unifying forces in the world" —*San Francisco Examiner*

Spiritual Travel

A WOMAN'S PATH
Women's Best Spiritual Travel Writing
Edited by Lucy McCauley, Amy G. Carlson & Jennifer Leo
ISBN 1-885-211-48-1
$16.95

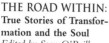

"A sensitive exploration of women's lives that have been unexpectedly and spiritually touched by travel experiences…highly recommended."
—*Library Journal*

THE ULTIMATE JOURNEY
Inspiring Stories of Living and Dying
James O'Reilly, Sean O'Reilly & Richard Sterling
ISBN 1-885-211-38-4
$17.95

"A glorious collection of writings about the ultimate adventure. A book to keep by one's bedside—and close to one's heart." —Philip Zaleski, editor, *The Best Spiritual Writing* series

THE ROAD WITHIN:
True Stories of Transformation and the Soul
Edited by Sean O'Reilly, James O'Reilly & Tim O'Reilly
ISBN 1-885-211-19-8
$17.95

— ★ ★ ★ —

Best Spiritual Book —Independent Publisher's Book Award

PILGRIMAGE
Adventures of the spirit
Edited by Sean O'Reilly & James O'Reilly
Introduction by Phil Cousineau
ISBN 1-885-211-56-2
$16.95

A diverse array of spirit-renewing journeys—trips to world-famous sites as well as places sacred, related by pilgrims of all kinds.

Adventure

TESTOSTERONE PLANET
True Stories from a Man's World
Edited by Sean O'Reilly, Larry Habegger & James O'Reilly
ISBN 1-885-211-43-0
$17.95

Thrills and laughter with some of today's best writers: Sebastian Junger, Tim Cahill, Bill Bryson, Jon Krakauer, and Frank McCourt.

DANGER!
True Stories of Trouble and Survival
Edited by James O'Reilly, Larry Habegger & Sean O'Reilly
ISBN 1-885-211-32-5
$17.95

"Exciting...for those who enjoy living on the edge or prefer to read the survival stories of others, this is a good pick." — *Library Journal*

Travel Humor

NOT SO FUNNY WHEN IT HAPPENED
The Best of Travel Humor and Misadventure
Edited by Tim Cahill
ISBN 1-885-211-55-4
$12.95

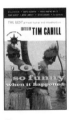

Laugh with Bill Bryson, Dave Barry, Anne Lamott, Adair Lara, Doug Lansky, and many more.

THERE'S NO TOILET PAPER...ON THE ROAD LESS TRAVELED
The Best of Travel Humor and Misadventure
Edited by Doug Lansky
ISBN 1-885-211-27-9
$12.95

—— ★ ★ ★ ——
Humor Book of the Year
—Independent Publisher's Book Award

Food

THE ADVENTURE OF FOOD
True Stories of Eating Everything
Edited by Richard Sterling
ISBN 1-885-211-37-6
$17.95

"These stories are bound to whet appetites for more than food."
—*Publishers Weekly*

FOOD
A Taste of the Road
Edited by Richard Sterling
Introduction by Margo True
ISBN 1-885-211-09-0
$17.95

Sumptious stories by M.F.K. Fisher, David Yeadon, P.J. O'Rourke, Colin Thubron, and many more.

—— ★ ★ ★ ——
Silver Medal Winner of the Lowell Thomas Award for Best Travel Book—Society of American Travel Writers

Special Interest

THE GIFT OF RIVERS
True Stories of Life on the Water
Edited by Pamela Michael
Introduction by Robert Hass
ISBN 1-885-211-42-2
$14.95

"*The Gift of Rivers* is a soulful fact- and image-filled compendium of wonderful stories that illuminate, educate, inspire and delight. One cannot read this compelling anthology without coming away in awe of the strong hold rivers exert on human imagination and history."
—David Brower, Chairman of Earth Island Institute

THE GIFT OF TRAVEL
The Best of Travelers' Tales
Edited by Larry Habegger, James O'Reilly & Sean O'Reilly
ISBN 1-885-211-25-2
$14.95

"Like gourmet chefs in a French market, the editors of Travelers' Tales pick, sift, and prod their way through the weighty shelves of contemporary travel writing, creaming off the very best."
—William Dalrymple, author of *City of Djinns*

FAMILY TRAVEL
The Farther You Go, the Closer You Get
Edited by Laura Manske
ISBN 1-885-211-33-3
$17.95

"This is family travel at its finest." —*Working Mother*

LOVE & ROMANCE
True Stories of Passion on the Road
Edited by Judith Babcock Wylie
ISBN 1-885-211-18-X
$17.95

"A wonderful book to read by a crackling fire."
—*Romantic Traveling*

THE GIFT OF BIRDS
True Encounters with Avian Spirits
Edited by Larry Habegger & Amy G. Carlson
ISBN 1-885-211-41-4
$17.95

"These are all wonderful, entertaining stories offering a *birds-eye view!* of our avian friends."
—*Booklist*

A DOG'S WORLD
True Stories of Man's Best Friend on the Road
Edited by Christine Hunsicker
ISBN 1-885-211-23-6
$12.95

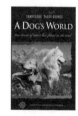

This extraordinary collection includes stories by John Steinbeck, Helen Thayer, James Herriot, Pico Iyer, and many others. A must for any dog and travel lover.

Submit Your Own Travel Tale

Do you have a tale of your own that you would like to submit to Travelers' Tales? For submission guidelines and a list of titles in the works, send a SASE to:

Travelers' Tales Submission Guidelines
330 Townsend Street, Suite 208, San Francisco, CA 94107

You may also send email to ***guidelines@travelerstales.com*** or visit our Web site at ***www.travelerstales.com***